f you take the best features of Mediterranean cuisine—fresh produce, lively flavors, approachable dishes—and swirl them with the finest traditions of central Europe—cured meats, delicious pickles—you have Armenian cuisine. Think skewered, roasted meats; a table laden with delicious side dishes, dips, and salads; hearty soups; grainy bowls; and thin, chewy lavash bread to wrap or scoop up every drop.

This book, part cookbook and part travelogue, takes you to a place as unexplored as you can find in modern times. Armenia is a land of kind people, tantalizing foods, strong spirits, and fascinating history. Many centuries ago, it is where trade paths merged, bringing together flavors from Europe, Asia, and the Middle East into a unique cuisine. It's where entire villages venture into the fields and hills to gather wild herbs, local lavash bakeries are social hubs, and every home has a stash of pickled vegetables.

Lavash features the many breads of Armenia—lavash, herb-stuffed jingalov hats, pizza-like lahmajo, focaccia-like matnakash—easy flatbreads you can prepare in your home kitchen. Then explore stuffed vegetables, salads, soups, sides, pickles, sweets, and meals for feasting, such as pumpkin stuffed with rice and dried fruit.

There is no finer way to understand a culture than to taste its foods. *Lavash* takes you through Armenia's gorgeous landscape, its proud and tragic history, and the hope of the now in more than 50 recipes and 100 photographs.

Lavash

Library of Congress Cataloging-in-Publication Data:

Names: Leahy, Kate, author. | Lee, John, author, photographer.
| Zada, Ara, author.
Title: Lavash : the bread that launched 1,000 meals, plus salads, stews, and other recipes from
Armenia / by Kate Leahy, John Lee, and Ara Zada ; photographs by John Lee.
Description: San Francisco : Chronicle Books, [2019] | Includes
bibliographical references and index.
Identifiers: LCCN 2018059141 | ISBN 9781452172651 (hardcover : alk. paper)
Subjects: LCSH: Lavash. | Cooking, Armenian. | LCGFT: Cookbooks.
Classification: LCC TX770.L38 L43 2019 | DDC 641.59566/2--dc23 LC record available at https://lccn.loc.gov/2018059141

Manufactured in China.

Prop and food styling by KATE LEAHY, JOHN LEE, and ARA ZADA.

Design by RACHEL HARRELL.

Ararat Exclusive Collection Yerevan Brandy Company Armenia is a registered trademark of Yerevan Brandy Company CJSC; Bactoferm is a registered trademark of CHR. HANSEN A/S; Coke is a registered trademark of The Coca-Cola Company; Diamond Crystal is a registered trademark of Cargill, Incorporated; Divina is a registered trademark of Mosaic Brands of New York, LLC; Instant Pot is a registered trademark of Instant Brands Inc.; Kalustyan is a registered trademark of Kalustyan Corporation; King Arthur is a registered trademark of King Arthur Flour Company, Inc.; KitchenAid is a registered trademark of Whirlpool Properties, Inc.; La Tourangelle is a registered trademark of Huilerie Croix Verte; Microplane is a registered trademark of Grace Manufacturing Inc.; Morton Salt is a registered trademark of Morton Salt, Inc.; Pernod Ricard is a registered trademark of Pernod Ricard Joint-Stock Company; Play-Doh is a registered trademark of Hasbro, Inc.; Pyrex is a registered trademark of Corning Incorporated; RapidRise is a registered trademark of AB Mauri Food, Inc.; Silpat is a registered trademark of ETS Guy DeMarle Joint Stock Company; Spectrum is a registered trademark of Spectrum Organic Products, LLC; Tetris is a registered trademark of Tetris Holding, LLC; Weber is a registered trademark of Weber-Stephen Products LLC; Wheatena is a registered trademark of Homestat Farm, Ltd. LLC; 99 Ranch is a registered trademark of Tawa Supermarket, Inc.

1 0 9 8 7 6 5 4 3 2

Chronicle books and gifts are available at special quantity discounts to corporations,
professional associations, literacy programs, and other organizations.
For details and discount information, please contact our premiums
department at corporatesales@chroniclebooks.com or at 1-800-759-0190.

Chronicle Books LLC
680 Second Street
San Francisco, California 94107
WWW.CHRONICLEBOOKS.COM

Lavash

The bread that launched 1,000 meals, plus salads, stews, and other recipes from Armenia

KATE LEAHY, JOHN LEE, and ARA ZADA

CONTENTS

Introduction

Around the Tonir
Flatbreads and Noodles

Creating Abundance
Sides and Simple Meals

Feasting

Khash, Khorovats, and
Heartier Dishes

A Summer's Thorn Is a Winter's Sweet

Fruit Preserves and Baked Treats

Introduction

The Lavash Bakers

Are we in the right place? We pull over in front of what's supposed to be Anna Tato-syan's bakery in the village of Argel. There's no sign, and all we see is an open garage door. But then we get out of the car and smell the wood smoke. Wearing a long dress covered with an apron and a pair of slippers, Anna pops out of the bakery to greet us, her round, rosy cheeks shining as she guides us inside, where a deep hole in the floor is filled with crackling logs. Made of clay, this is the bakery's *tonir*, a type of subterranean oven that Armenians have used for centuries for baking bread and heating homes. When the logs burn down to embers, four women with their hair tied back in bandanas get to work around the tonir, wielding balls of dough like professional baseball players warming up before a game. These are Anna's lavash bakers.

Lusine Abrahamyan lobs a piece of dough to Aida Beyboutyan, who flattens it into a smooth sheet with a rolling pin before passing it to Liana Grigoryan. With a sturdy brown apron covering her sweatpants, Liana is the team's no-nonsense slugger. She frowns, spins the dough in the air, stretching it paper-thin before draping it over what looks like an uncomfortably firm pillow. It actually isn't a pillow at all but a straw-filled pad called a *batat*, which gives traditional lavash its long, oval shape. With one decisive swoop, Liana strikes the batat against the wall of the tonir. The dough sticks on contact and begins to puff and blister. After a minute, Hasmik Khachatryan fishes out the lavash with a hook, turns it over to quickly sear the other side, and then stacks it beside her. Flecked with blisters, this is classic tonir lavash, and it's stunning to behold.

It's only after the bakers take a coffee break that Liana's frown relaxes and we start to look around the bakery, taking in the stone walls blackened with ash and lined with bags of flour, the cherry-red, Soviet-era scale, and the abacus used by store manager Nara Ivanyan to make change for purchases. Then we begin asking questions: How much salt is in the dough? Do you add yeast? How long does the dough rest before you bake it?

Before we can query any more, Liana retreats to the kitchen, returning with a pot of just-boiled potatoes, pickled beets, and pickled green peppers. She tears off a piece of lavash, wraps it around a potato, sprinkles salt on top, and hands it to us.

We look at each other—potatoes wrapped in bread with nothing else? Our California minds scan the room for hot sauce. Yet the yellow, waxy potatoes taste as if they were basted in butter and the lavash is still warm, with a crisp-soft crust. These potato wraps are improbable home runs, confirming that traveling across countless time zones to eat lavash in Armenia has been well worth it.

Women (and it's nearly always women) bake lavash all over Armenia much like the bakers we met in Argel, a village about twenty minutes away from Yerevan, the country's capital. By making this traditional flatbread, which is eaten daily at almost every meal in the country, they're also preserving history. Lavash is so important to Armenia that UNESCO added it to its intangible cultural heritage list in 2014.

The journey that brought the three of us—John Lee, Ara Zada, and me, Kate Leahy—to Anna's bakery, and into homes, markets, and restaurants across Armenia, started in 2015. That summer, John, a photographer from San Francisco, taught a food photography course in Yerevan at the TUMO Center for Creative Technologies, an organization providing free after-school workshops for Armenian students on subjects ranging from art and animation to robotics. It was on that trip that he discovered lavash—earth-shattering lavash, he called it. Back home, he told everyone about it.

I was one of those people. While working together on a different project, John filled me in on his trip, flipping through images he took with the students. Years earlier, I had studied the link between food and Armenian-American identity for a college thesis, mining for stories in self-published cookbooks, Armenian church bazaars, and the California State Archives. But after John finished his informal slideshow, I realized that I didn't recognize any of the dishes from those beloved Armenian-American church bazaars or community cookbooks. Instead, I saw mulberries collected on a bedsheet in an orchard, trout strung up to dry on the shores of Lake Sevan, and outdoor tables covered with plates of roasted vegetables bathed in dappled sunlight. It felt new and familiar all at once, a foundational way of eating that cultures around the world have adapted and made their own. I also knew that I had never eaten the kind of lavash that John was talking about.

Through TUMO's global network, we met Ara Zada, a chef in Southern California. In 2016, he taught a culinary workshop for TUMO, working new techniques into Armenian dishes. Ara grew up in an Armenian-Egyptian household in Los Angeles, attending Armenian school through seventh grade. But the food he encountered in Yerevan was different—Armenian, sure, but not what he had at home. As a kid, he ate more pita bread than lavash, and he had never heard of Panrkhash (page 201), a layered lavash bake that has more in common with mac and cheese than anything from Alice Bezjian's *The Complete Armenian Cookbook*—the book that his mom (and every other Armenian mom in Southern California) used. He wanted to learn more about the food of *Hayastan*, what Armenians call their country.

The three of us cobbled together a culinary recon mission that involved traveling to Armenia and documenting how to make this bread—and other forms of *hats* (Armenian for "bread")—as well as what to eat with it. We met a mix of experts: chefs from establishments such as Tufenkian Old Dilijan Complex in Dilijan and Old Armenia in Gyumri, as well as home cooks throughout Armenia and the Republic of Artsakh. And every time we found a bakery, we walked in, introduced ourselves, and chatted with the bakers. A skeptical reader might wonder why anyone was willing to share trade secrets with three outsiders like us, but while traveling in Armenia and corresponding from California, we encountered extreme generosity and patience, meeting people who wanted to share their recipes merely because we asked.

The stories in this book are not only about food but also about Armenia, a tiny republic in the South Caucasus that today sits at a crossroads between its Soviet past and an uncertain (but promising) future. Rather than a definitive guide, this book is a collection of dispatches from the road, of the flavors and foods that stayed with us after traveling in this immensely hospitable country. These stories are tributes to a nation of makers, of adaptable people who have lived through times where the only way to guarantee a stable source of food was to produce it yourself.

In this context, lavash fits perfectly with that adaptability. Need a soup spoon? Shape a piece of lavash into a scoop to help slurp up broth. Need to keep your soup hot? Cover it with a piece of lavash. Need a takeout container for your *khorovats* (grilled meats and vegetables)? Bundle the grilled goods in one big sheet of lavash. Need a break from lavash? Dry it out and store it for later, then spritz it with water to bring it back to life. But in all honesty, we have yet to find a need to take a break from lavash.

Armenian Food

Beyond lavash, what *is* Armenian food? Well, it's complicated.

The collection of recipes in this book represents the dishes we sampled on our travels within Armenia, the ones that we came to love and could re-create back home with ingredients that are easy to find, such as fresh herbs, cucumbers, tomatoes, eggs, and yogurt. Many of the dishes in this book may be unfamiliar to those who know Armenian food outside of Armenia, and some might wonder why their favorite Armenian-American recipes are missing. The truth is that Armenia itself represents a homeland shared by people with very different histories and food traditions. These differences became much more pronounced in the twentieth century, when Armenians in the west were displaced due to genocide while Armenians in the east became Soviet citizens. Over time, diaspora communities evolved separately from Soviet Armenia and both adapted to their very different political and social situations, absorbing new food influences as well. While Armenians around the world still make the cured meat Basturma (page 138), stuffed vegetable Summer Tolma (page 178), and various kinds of baklava (page 239), Armenians in Armenia also embrace Soviet foods, like Salat Vinaigrette (page 95), a hearty salad, as well as potatoes, sour cream, and vodka.

As members of the diaspora move to Armenia, however, they are bringing their traditions with them and broadening the scope of what Armenian food in Hayastan can be. Some recipes in this book, such as Lahmajo ("Armenian pizza," also known as *lahmajoon*, page 64) and Chikufta (page 126), a steak tartare–style preparation, are examples of this evolution. Other recipes we've included, like Harissa (page 196), a porridge made of wheat berries cooked with a little meat, are much older, with roots in an ancient Armenian nation that once was much larger. Still others, like *murabba* (page 226), a type of fruit preserve eaten throughout the Caucasus and Middle East, speak to cultural exchanges that have taken place in this part of the world for centuries.

Just because a dish is important to Armenia doesn't mean that it is exclusive to Armenia, and we have no intention of untangling politically charged "who made it first" stories. Instead, we focus on what's grown and made in the country today. In the spring, that means heaps of fresh greens, much of it wild, while in the summer, it's about fruit, from plums, cherries, and grapes to the country's famous apricots, all of which are dried or preserved in various ways. In the fall, next to boxes of apples and quince are persimmons from Meghri, a city near the Iranian border, and the market stalls fill with potatoes, cabbage, carrots, walnuts, and dried fruit.

Like apricots, pomegranates are also a universal symbol of Armenia, important enough through the ages that they were carved into the doors of monasteries—nearly always next to bunches of grapes, another celebrated crop. On the table,

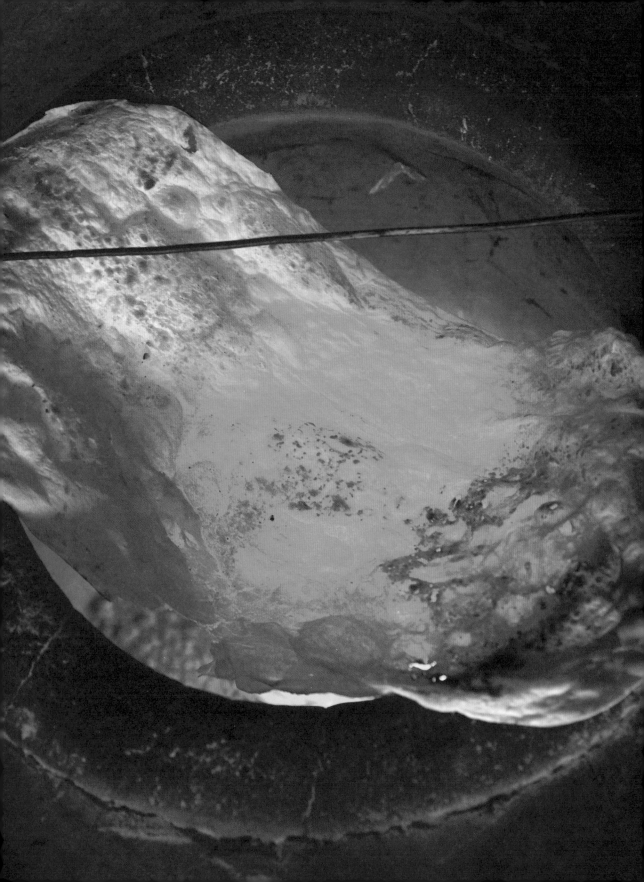

pomegranate seeds can be eaten for dessert, sprinkled over main courses, like Lavash-Wrapped Trout (page 183), for color, or folded into the herb filling of the flatbread Jingalov Hats (page 58). All year round, there's no escaping tomatoes and cucumbers, which are grown in greenhouses in cold months. And no matter what time of the year, a bouquet of fresh herbs—flat-leaf parsley, cilantro, dill, and opal basil—is part of every meal. Fresh herbs are so prevalent that we could have ended every ingredient list in this book with "handful of mixed herbs, chopped." This is how important they are to recreating Hayastantsi flavor.

There is an enduring belief that the best food of all is what's made at home. Whether they live in Yerevan or in the countryside, Armenian cooks pick wild greens in the spring, make pickles in the summer, and cure *basturma* in the fall. On one crisp November day in 2017, we visited a home in Yeghvard, a town outside of Yerevan. Neighborhood women had gathered in the back of the house around the tonir to help bake lavash, keeping the fire hot by feeding it scrap pieces of wood. Sheets of bread already lay on the roof and in the hallways to dry. The women explained that they stack and store the lavash in a spare bedroom to keep for winter when it's too cold to fire up the tonir, sprinkling it with water to soften the bread before eating. It's this act of preserving, whether it's applied to bread, meat, vegetables, or fruit, that creates the backbone of the Armenian table.

Armenian History

To understand the food in Armenia today, it helps to know how this small country in the South Caucasus evolved out of a much larger nation.

Founded in 1991 after the collapse of the Soviet Union, the Republic of Armenia is slightly larger than Massachusetts but with half the population. Although small, Armenia's high-altitude landscape is diverse, bringing to mind stretches of the American West mixed with California's agricultural Central Valley and the forests of Vermont. Lake Sevan, the largest body of water in this landlocked country, sits at 6,234 feet [1900 m] above sea level, and in the fall its shores are speckled orange with sea buckthorn berries. On a clear day, the capital city of Yerevan has unobstructed views of the two snow-capped peaks of Mount Ararat, the resting place (according to legend) of Noah's ark. That Mount Ararat, a lasting symbol of Armenia, lies in Turkey is a heartbreaking reminder that the epic history of Armenia is complex, tragic, heroic—and still unfolding.

Historic Armenia—also called the Armenian Highlands and the Armenian Plateau by writers and historians throughout the ages—has been a specific geographical location since antiquity, at one point covering a swath of land between the Black, Caspian, and

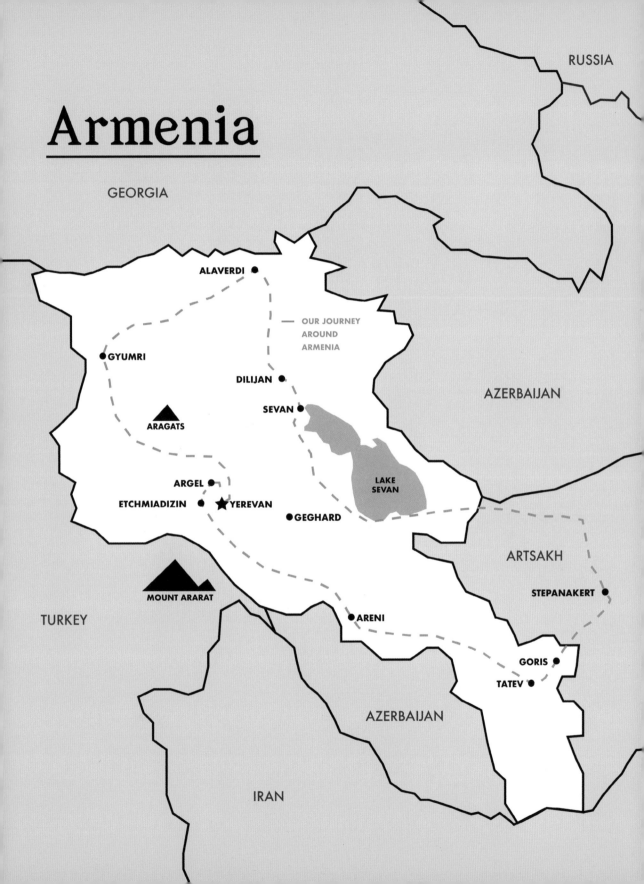

Armenia

RUSSIA

GEORGIA

● ALAVERDI

OUR JOURNEY
AROUND
ARMENIA

● GYUMRI

● DILIJAN

AZERBAIJAN

● SEVAN

▲ ARAGATS

LAKE
SEVAN

● ARGEL

ETCHMIADIZIN ● ★ YEREVAN

● GEGHARD

ARTSAKH

▲ MOUNT ARARAT

STEPANAKERT ●

TURKEY

● ARENI

GORIS ●

TATEV ●

AZERBAIJAN

IRAN

Mediterranean seas. Armenia emerged out of the ancient Urartu civilization, first in the sixth century B.C., before falling under Achaemenid rule, and later in the second century B.C. In the early fourth century A.D., Armenia became the first nation to adopt Christianity as its religion. Religion would not only change Armenia's spiritual practices but also its politics, culture, and written word. It was the drive to spread the gospel that prompted Mesrop Mashtots to create the first written Armenian alphabet in the fifth century A.D. Today, this patron saint of language is immortalized with a tree-lined boulevard in central Yerevan dead-ending at the Matenadaran, a library devoted to ancient books that is dedicated to him.

Language and religion differentiated Armenians from their neighbors, yet the Armenian people were also skilled at building multicultural trading networks along the land routes of the Silk Road, which happened to cut through Armenia. This geographic advantage had a downside, though, making the nation a prized acquisition for everyone from the Romans and Mongols to the Persians, Turks, and Russians. It was constant pressure from various empire builders that eventually led to the fall of the last major Armenian kingdom in A.D. 1045, and Armenians wouldn't regain statehood within their historic homeland until the twentieth century. Perhaps common Armenian phrases, such as *tsavet tanem* ("let me take your pain"), which conveys a friendly attitude, evolved out of the nation's constant struggle for survival.

Eastern and Western Armenia

Many of the differences between the way that Armenians of the diaspora cook (with olive oil, spices, and—as Ara says—a lot of lemon juice on everything) and the way Armenians in Armenia cook (with seed oils, mild paprika, and sparing use of apple cider vinegar) emerged in the twentieth century. But the foundation for this division came about as early as the eleventh century.

The fall of the last Armenian kingdom in historic Armenia gave rise to the Armenian Kingdom of Cilicia, which established itself away from the highlands and along the Eastern Mediterranean coast. Aligning itself with the European Crusaders, Cilicia flourished for three centuries as a coastal kingdom and center of trade for everything from raw silks to spices, raisins, and wine. Although the kingdom fell in the fourteenth century, eventually becoming part of the Ottoman Empire, the cities within it retained Armenian communities and Eastern Mediterranean character well into the early twentieth century.

Meanwhile, from the Middle Ages on, control of historic Armenia bounced between several powers, most significantly the Ottoman sultans and the Persian shahs. In 1639, the Treaty of Zuhab granted some respite from war, giving the South Caucasus to Persia and everything west of it to the Ottoman Empire. After the treaty took effect, foreign travelers began using the phrases "Western" or "Turkish" Armenia for Ottoman-controlled Armenia and "Eastern" or "Persian" Armenia to refer to the portion of Armenia under the control of the shahs. While foundational foods, such as lavash, harissa, and yogurt, were eaten on both sides of the split, Eastern Armenians were also influenced by Persian traditions. Yet across historic Armenia, food was simple: a good meal consisted of bread, butter, yogurt, and cheese served with greens, while rice and meat were delicacies. By the nineteenth century, a declining Persian Empire opened the door for another power to take control, and Eastern Armenia become part of the Russian Empire.

By the twentieth century, Armenians living in Eastern Armenia and elsewhere within Imperial Russia faced wildly different fates than those in Western Armenia, who endured an increasingly precarious existence as Christian minorities under the Ottoman Empire. At the same time, instability and famine across Eastern and Western historic Armenia prompted those with enough resources to migrate to cities. The most prosperous joined the communities of Armenian merchants, artisans, and intellectuals in Constantinople in the west and Tbilisi (called Tiflis by Armenians) and Moscow in the east. While city life preserved Armenian culture, geographical and political differences also furthered the gap between the west and east.

1915

Beginning in 1915, a river of Armenian refugees fleeing the Ottoman Empire began arriving in Yerevan, then a multicultural though provincial outpost of the Russian Empire, which was on the brink of collapse. The reason for the arrivals: massacres on a scale that had never been seen before.

It was not the first time in modern history that Armenians had been the targets of violence. In the late nineteenth century, rumors of Armenian insurgencies led to the killings of thousands of Armenians in villages and Constantinople. While political shake-ups within the Ottoman Empire in 1908 and 1913 offered hope for greater equality and democracy, it soon became evident that the new rulers, the "Three Pashas"—Ismail Enver, Ahmed Djemal, and Mehmed Talaat—sought to promote the idea of a superior Turkish race at the devastating expense of minorities within the empire.

After the Ottoman Empire entered World War I as a German ally, Talaat, the minister of the interior, used the guise of homeland security to justify rounding up Armenian civilians. By the spring of 1915, a pattern emerged across the empire: Armenian men were called out of cities and villages and then shot or hung. The next day, the women and children were ordered to pack whatever they could carry so officials could move them to safer places. A secretive government force made up of former prisoners accompanied by a military escort would then either kill the women and children or

The Year of The Sword

Growing up Armenian in America, I was constantly reminded about the Armenian genocide. I remember sitting with my dede, grandfather, the first time he told me the story of what happened to our family. Afterward, he rarely missed an opportunity to remind me, raising a finger in front of his face, pointing to the sky and, with a stern voice, saying, "My grandfather, God rest his soul, was from Mardin!"

In the early 1900s, my great-great-grandfather Farosh Manooshian was a well-known artist in Mardin, a once-peaceful city perched on a rocky hill in what is today southeastern Turkey. But despite stories from my grandfather, the scope of what happened to make Farosh leave his hometown never really hit me until I set foot in the Genocide Memorial and Museum at Tsitsernakaberd in Yerevan. The cold, gray concrete walls were filled with images of death and torture, telling stories of soldiers who killed thousands of men, women, and children as if it were a game. As I stared at images of bodies piled up, I began to realize that the only reason I was standing in this room was because some of my family members were among those who survived.

Over the years, I've pieced together more of what happened to my great-great-grandfather. Leading up to 1915, the people of Mardin had a tradition of banding together no matter their race or religion. The governor of Mardin at the time, who had always viewed Muslims and Christians as equals, refused Ottoman orders to turn in Armenian citizens. His refusal cost him his life and the lives of his ranked officers. The next governor stuck to the Ottoman script and began carrying out orders to deport and murder all Armenians in the city. In Mardin, this time became known as "the year of the sword" for the countless Armenians who were marched through the city and massacred while everyone watched.

Since my great-great-grandfather had a reputation as an artist, however, he was told that his family's lives would be spared as long as he continued working on a painting inside a mosque. The night before he finished, a soldier who had been guarding him—and who had become a friend—told him that he and his family would be murdered the next morning if he stayed. That soldier helped him flee with his family in the dead of night. They traveled by mule to Syria and then to the city of Tafilah in Jordan, eventually making their way to Cairo, where he changed the family's last name from Manooshian to Zada to avoid more persecution. Since my great-great-grandfather spoke Arabic, he fit in easily with his Egyptian neighbors, though he didn't forget his heritage.

As my kids grow older, I will make sure that they, like me, learn the same story that my grandfather told me and that they understand their heritage. It's up to us and every Armenian to preserve our culture and honor those who lost their lives more than a century ago. We are the survivors.

—Ara Zada

force them to march into the Syrian desert toward Aleppo. Many died of dehydration and starvation, while others were picked off along the way.

A genocide does two things, explains Noubar Afeyan, a founder of the Aurora Humanitarian Initiative, which supports those who fight genocide around the world: It wipes out an entire group of people—those who are killed—and it destroys a nation by dispersing and disconnecting those who survive. An estimated 1.5 million Armenians, as well as thousands of Greeks and Assyrians, lost their lives between 1915 and 1918. Those who weren't killed were displaced from their homes forever, most of them moving far from historic Armenia or the former Kingdom of Cilicia. To this day, the Turkish government denies that the Armenian genocide occurred.

Armenians did persevere, though. Diaspora communities grew in Egypt, Lebanon, Syria, France, America, and beyond. And although reduced in size, a corner of Armenia's historic territory was gained back—with some help from the Soviet Union.

Soviet Years

From 1917, following the collapse of the Russian Empire, to 1920, Armenia tried to establish itself as an independent country. But without the wealthy Armenian community of Tbilisi, which was part of Georgia, the new republic was left with a poor countryside surrounding then-small Yerevan. And Yerevan was filling up with refugees from Western Armenia who desperately needed food and shelter. (In the United States, a famous post–World War I campaign to send aid to Armenia urged Americans to "remember the starving Armenians.") By 1920, only 720,000 Armenians lived in Eastern Armenia, and nearly half of them were refugees. The country was once again vulnerable to takeover, which came with the arrival of Lenin's Red Army.

Soviet rule significantly changed the course of Armenian history, both politically and culturally. In the 1920s, as Armenia occupied itself with feeding its people, Moscow ceded the land west of the Arax River, including Mount Ararat, to Turkey and granted Nagorno Karabakh, an ethnically Armenian province (called Artsakh in ancient times and by Armenians today), to Azerbaijan, which was economically stronger. These actions not only removed Armenia's most iconic mountain from Armenia, but also eventually led to war in the 1990s with Azerbaijan over Nagorno Karabakh, a conflict that remains unresolved (see Artsakh, page 85).

Socially, the Soviet Union further divided the culture within Armenia from that of Armenians elsewhere in the world. An agricultural state became an urban one, and entire villages moved from rural settings into Soviet apartments to work at factories or state-run farms. Yerevan was transformed entirely from a scruffy trading outpost into a Soviet-style city, with broad boulevards and buildings constructed from the pink tufa

rock. On a hillside, a statue of Stalin glowered at the population, seeming to compel Armenians to learn Russian. (The statue has since been replaced with another Soviet monument, Mother Armenia.)

There was also an effect on food and drink. After surviving decades of hunger, Soviet Armenia's food supplies stabilized through central planning. Prior to World War I, Russians had been unsuccessful in introducing pork to Yerevan, where butcher shops mostly sold lamb. During the Soviet era, however, the preference flipped, and even today, pork and beef are more popular than lamb. Also, despite having a heritage of winemaking that goes back to prehistoric times (see Ancient Wine in the Twenty-First Century, page 213), Armenians were discouraged from producing wine. Grapes once used for wine became earmarked for Armenian brandy production—Georgians made enough wine, the Soviets reasoned. Somewhat ironically, the man credited as the architect of the Soviet food industry was Anastas Mikoyan, an Armenian born near the Georgian border and one of the few members of Stalin's inner circle who lived long enough to enjoy a peaceful retirement. Among the commissar's many contributions to the Soviet table, one of the most lasting was publishing *The Book of Tasty and Healthy Food*, a cookbook first released in 1939 offering recipes ranging from stuffed cabbage to fish in aspic. With millions of copies and countless editions in print today, the book came to define aspirational Soviet home cooking.

Cookbooks were one form of Soviet propaganda; another was a campaign encouraging Armenians to move to Soviet Armenia. Beginning in the 1940s, messages proclaiming a bountiful, welcoming land reached diaspora communities, encouraging those from Aleppo, Beirut, Cairo, America, and elsewhere to resettle in a country that served as a link to the historic highlands. Those who came, however, found they had neither a job nor a place to live upon arrival. They also didn't speak Armenian exactly the same way (see Language Lessons, page 27) and they bemoaned the lack of spices in the local food. They were called *akhpars* (slang derived from the word *yeghbayr*, Armenian for "brother"), which rather than being a welcoming gesture, further pointed to the newcomers' differences. Lahmajo (page 64), the popular flatbread topped with ground meat eaten everywhere in Yerevan today, was an exotic akhpar food in mid-century Soviet Armenia. These repatriates also helped open up Armenia to other new foods. One woman told us that it was an akhpar neighbor from Cairo who first introduced her to zucchini, a squash she had never seen as a child.

It wasn't all bad, though, and certain Soviet foods became beloved. Every mom in Armenia knows how to make Salat Vinaigrette (page 95), a classic Russian salad of boiled beets, beans, and potatoes. *Smetana*, Russian sour cream, is common in cooking and baking, and caviar and trout roe became delicacies. Every kitchen also seems to be outfitted with the same Soviet-era meat grinder. Grinding meat at home instead of buying it already ground from a butcher is a habit that Armenians from Armenia, even those who later move away, never lose. And old traditions didn't die out. The same people who moved to apartments returned to their villages to collect fruit from mulberry trees or forage for wild greens and herbs. While Soviets tried to downplay the value of lavash in exchange for thicker breads, the tradition of baking lavash in a tonir never stopped, and villages like Argel, with reputations for lavash, became required stops for picking up provisions on the way to spend the weekend at a *dacha* (no-frills vacation home).

New Armenia

On our trips to Armenia, we witnessed a country in transition, especially around Yerevan, where a new generation of Armenians from Europe and America are putting down roots to help rebuild the country. Diaspora Armenians are investing in the wine industry, creating tech startups, and aiding with infrastructure projects, while Syrian Armenians displaced by war are reinvigorating the local restaurant scene, offering polished hospitality and Middle Eastern flavors that are a break from the state-run restaurants of the past. Politically, Armenia is also changing rapidly. In 2018, peaceful protests across the country succeeded in ousting unpopular prime minister Serzh Sargsyan and putting Nikol Pashinyan, a highly popular opposition leader, in power, kicking off a wave of reforms.

Yet some older residents are nostalgic for the Soviet years. On April 24, 2018, Remembrance Day, as we walked along with thousands of others to pay tribute at the Tsitsernakaberd Genocide Memorial in Yerevan, an older woman behind us lamented the rise of materialism in Armenia. It used to be that no one knew what they were missing, that they were all the same, she said. Part of the reason for the nostalgia stems from fresh memories of the difficult times that followed the collapse of the USSR. Under the Soviet Union, Armenia became a hub for engineers and physicists. Yerevan's art scene also flourished. In contrast, in 1991 the republic became a tiny independent country without the infrastructure to deliver basic needs. In those dark days, kerosene and bread were handed out by international aid organizations, and sometimes all there was to eat was bread and water, which cooks turned into Konchol (page 108), a soup flavored with caramelized onions, chopped herbs, and an egg, if you were lucky. Those who were kids in Yerevan in the 1990s remember bracingly cold winters and their parents' attempts to distract them by playing games or instruments, or encouraging dancing to keep warm. When the lights flickered on for a rare few hours, the entire city celebrated.

There are different challenges today. During the Soviet era, one kept the same factory job for life. But in an Armenia that wants to participate in global trade, employers require more flexible skills, and some people feel left behind. The problem was not lost on the diaspora, which was how the TUMO Center for Creative Technologies came to be. Armenian-Texan philanthropist Sam Simonian and his wife, Sylva, founded TUMO in Yerevan in 2011 with a mission to close the education gap with technology and creative endeavors. Thousands of Armenian teenagers have since taken TUMO's after-school workshops led by pioneers in robotics, film, graphics, music, food, and writing. The same grandmothers who miss the old days are proud of their grandkids, the TUMO generation, who will be the ones to lead change in the country.

These days, whenever we find ourselves chatting with anyone—Armenian or not—who has traveled through the country, we end up sharing this little excited smile with each other. It's like we're in on a secret, pulling a fast one on the rest of the travelers of the world, who tick through the obvious international tourist spots, dodging selfie sticks while enduring greatest-hits menus. In this place between Europe, Asia, and the Middle East, the ancient sites become open-air museums set against dramatic terrain, and the hospitality is honest and gracious. And these days, there is also always plenty of lavash to go around.

Language Lessons

When researching this book, we grappled not only with writing Armenian words in Roman letters but also differentiating between Western and Eastern Armenian pronunciations. The tricky part is that some sounds don't exist in English and the phonetics are interpreted differently depending on who is doing the translating. Typically, the letter "p" in Western Armenian becomes an Eastern Armenian "b" (paklava to baklava), a last name ending in "-ian" is more often spelled "-yan," the letter "k" becomes the letter "g" (kata to gata), and the letter "d" becomes a "t" (dolma to tolma). We once had trouble tracking down a khorovats place in Yerevan that we thought was called Daron only to find that the sign out front read "Taron." Getting Romanized spellings for Eastern Armenian names was also a challenge, but we found Eastern Armenians were incredibly easygoing about it. Ask them which spelling is right—d or t, b or p? "Whichever you prefer!" is nearly always the answer. In other words, as you read this book, allow some room for, shall we say, interpretation.

Cooking from This Book

In the recipes we include in this book, we sought to re-create the spirit of the food we ate with ingredients we could find where we live. With some exceptions, we focus on widely available ingredients, from parsley, cilantro, and green onions to yogurt, tomatoes, cucumbers, and potatoes. Most Armenian recipes are purposefully simple, with little to hide behind, so their success can depend on the quality of the ingredients. The descriptions that follow explain what we look for when shopping for ingredients and how we use them.

On Dairy

The butter, cheese, and yogurt made in Armenia all have the advantage of starting with high-quality local milk. When using this book, look for the best dairy products you can buy for the best results.

BUTTER The texture and flavor of Armenian butter is rich and reminiscent of more famous European butters. The best butter changes with the season, turning from creamy pale in winter to rich yellow in May and June when the cows graze on wildflowers. Most of the butter used is unsalted, because people are choosy about the quality of the butter and because salted butters in Soviet times were inferior. Yerevan local Tatev Malkhasyan's family makes salted butter by pressing a layer of softened butter in the bottom of a cast-iron pan, covering it with a layer of salt, and repeating the process a few more times. They let the butter sit for a couple of days in a cold place until it releases water, then they remove the water and melt the butter until it's clear, with a thin layer of foam on the surface. At that point, they boil the butter until the foam is gone. When cool, it's packed into jars. Both clarified butter and whole butter are used in cooking and sweets.

CHEESE The most common cheeses in Armenia are salt-brined cheeses with holes—"eyes" in the language of cheesemaking. The more sour the milk, the larger the eyes.

While the two most common cheeses—*Lori* and *chanakh*—are used interchangeably, Lori is firmer and chanakh is saltier, explains Robert Ghazaryan, a cheesemaker and farmer in the northern Lori region who makes both cheeses with local cow's milk. Sheep's milk feta, such as the French cheese Valbreso, comes close to the salty, funky tang of these cheeses, and it makes a good addition to any herb and cheese plate served with the recipes in this book.

Other Armenian cheeses include Chechil, which is similar to string cheese in America (though with finer strands), and a few funkier creations for the more adventurous. If you're looking to try one of these more adventurous cheeses while visiting Armenia, ask to sample *motal*, a goat cheese packed into clay pots and sealed with beeswax, or an aged cheese buried for several months with herbs, a style attributed to the town of Yeghegnadzor. For many, the pungent, barnyard-like flavor is an acquired taste, though others can't get enough.

YOGURT (MADZOON) Long before yogurt became a probiotic elixir in the United States, Eastern and Western Armenians alike had long credited eating yogurt with living a healthier life. Neighbors borrow a bit of madzoon from each other to culture a new batch of fresh milk. To prepare for winter, some Armenian women dry disks of defatted yogurt mixed with a little flour in the sun to keep on hand for when cows aren't producing milk. Called *chortan* or *choratan*, this dried yogurt is turned into yogurt soup in the winter. When it comes to fresh yogurt in Armenia, it is always whole-milk (full-fat), plain yogurt, and some are thicker than others. In this book, yogurt is often mixed with a little grated garlic, which is great on noodles or drizzled over greens, as is done in "Aveluk Salad" (page 100). Yogurt is not hard to make at home, but it takes time. For a more in-depth look at making yogurt, look for cookbooks on the subject by writers Janet Fletcher and Cheryl Sternman Rule.

DRINKING YOGURT: A popular way to cool off in the summer is to drink a thinned-out, savory-style yogurt drink called *tan* or *tahn*. Pair it with the "Armenian pizza" Lahmajo (page 64) for lunch. The thickness of tan and whether you add mint to the glass is a personal preference.

To try it for yourself, use a fork to whisk ¼ cup [60 g] plain, whole-milk yogurt in a glass with ¾ cup [180 ml] water and ¼ tsp salt. You can add a little chopped mint, though purists leave it out.

On Produce

One of the reasons that vegetables and fruit taste so vibrant in Armenia is that most produce is grown locally. The Ararat Valley is the backbone of Armenia's agriculture, and it's close to Yerevan. There are also small village farmers around the country that drive their produce into the capital city to sell at a higher margin.

In the spring, tart green plums the size of large cherries (*shlor*) begin to pop up, while in summer, boxes of stone fruits and eggplants crowd stalls. In the fall, quince, walnuts, dried fruit, cauliflower, and cabbage take their places. Greenhouses now make it possible to have tomatoes and cucumbers year-round. One clarification on cucumbers: Those eaten throughout Armenia resemble what Americans call Persian cucumbers, not what we call Armenian cucumbers. Those large, pale-green vegetables are technically a type of melon.

GARLIC AND ONIONS Raw, cooked, pickled, or charred on a grill, garlic and onions are foundational flavors in Armenian cooking. To reduce garlic's pungency, mix minced or grated garlic cloves with salt. Armenian green onions are much skinnier than American green onions (also called scallions), with a more delicate flavor. If the green onions you have are large, slice them in half lengthwise before serving them on an herb and cheese plate. Once you cut off the roots, use both the white and the green parts of the green onion. The other onion used frequently in this book is the everyday yellow onion. They vary quite a bit in size, but some variance is fine. In general, the yellow onions we use weigh approximately 8.75 oz [250 g] each and equal about 2 cups [480 ml] finely diced or 2½ cups [600 ml] sliced. For all kinds of onions, soaking raw slices in cold water or in a mix of water and any kind of vinegar helps dilute the astringency and makes them more pleasant to eat raw. When recipes call for finely diced onion, you can also grate the onion using a box grater.

DRIED FRUIT The combination of local harvests, dry summers, and three hundred days of sunshine makes Armenia ideal for drying fruit. The most celebrated is the apricot—what the Romans called *Prunus armenicus*, Armenian plum. Today, apricots, both fresh and dried, remain a symbol of Armenia, but dried *hon* (cornelian cherries) and dried sour plums are also favorite snacks. For this book, dried sour cherries best approximate hon, and prunes paired with vinegar or another tart ingredient substitute for sour plums. Together, they make for nice combinations in stuffed rice dishes, like Ghapama (page 186).

On Grains and Beans

Bread wheat, emmer, and barley have been farmed in the Ararat Valley since the Neolithic era, later becoming an important part of the Armenian diet. The importance of wheat didn't diminish during the Soviet era, but it shifted. Wheat remained the most important cereal crop grown in the USSR, but from the 1950s on, most of it was grown in the Russian Federation and Kazakhstan. Nowadays, Armenia grows wheat and emmer, while barley is mostly grown for livestock. On the other hand, the delicious speckled beans that grow around the city of Goris are a New World crop. Rice is also popular in Armenia, but it is imported.

WHEAT BERRIES AND FARRO Wheat berries are milled into flour and cooked in a range of porridges. Some are toasted and crushed for Khashil (page 193), others cooked low and slow for Harissa (page 196) and Kurkut (page 198), and still others processed into bulgur. Occasionally, emmer (also called farro) is used, but not as often. Go to a shop in Armenia and you'll be able to pick out wheat berries specifically processed for the dish you're making. In America, we have to get a little more creative.

Pearled farro replicates the texture of the wheat berries used in harissa and is easy to find (it is also sometimes labeled *farro perlato*, the Italian translation). White wheat berries, such as Sonora, are softer, and work well for dishes like harissa. Kurkut, a porridge from the Republic of Artsakh, uses a type of hard red winter wheat berry. To replicate it, we use unpearled farro or Turkey Red wheat berries, which (contrary to their name) were brought to America by Mennonites from the Ukraine. When cooking wheat berries, use 4 cups [960 ml] water to 1 cup [180 g] wheat berries. For faster cooking, soak wheat berries overnight and drain before using.

BULGUR Made by boiling, drying, and grinding wheat, bulgur is quite different from whole or crushed wheat berries and isn't a substitute for them. In this book, it's used as a filling for Pasuts Tolma (page 174) and as part of raw beef preparation Chikufta (page 126) and its vegetarian cousin, Eech (page 129). Use medium-grain bulgur, also called "#2."

RICE Buttery rice *plov* (pilaf) most likely reached Armenia through connections on the Silk Road, but it never displaced cooked wheat berries, which were easier to grow in Armenia's arid climate. For that reason, rice was historically a delicacy. Besides plov, rice is an integral part of stuffed vegetable dishes, such as Grape Leaf Tolma (page 171) and Ghapama (page 186). For the recipes in this book where rice is used, opt for any long-grain variety of white rice.

BEANS The southern Armenian city of Goris and the villages that surround it are famous for their speckled, purple-magenta shelling beans. The beans' vibrant colors dull when they're cooked, but what they lose in appearance they gain in flavor and their creamy-on-the-inside, chewy-on-the-outside texture. To best approximate Goris beans, look for cranberry beans, also called borlotti beans. While it is easier to find these beans dried, they are also available canned in some

stores, especially those stocked with Italian and Mediterranean ingredients. Though slightly smaller, dried or canned pinto beans are good substitutes.

COOKING DRIED BEANS: Rinse the beans and pick out any debris. Place the beans in a bowl and cover generously with water. Let soak for at least 4 hours or overnight. This presoaking step yields evenly cooked beans that are supposed to be easier on the digestive system (though not everyone agrees it makes a difference). If an overnight soak is not in the cards, you can also do the "quick soak" method: Place the beans in a large pot and cover generously with water. Bring the pot to a boil, turn off the heat, and let sit, uncovered, for about 1 hour. Once the beans are soaked, drain the beans, put them back in the pot, and add water to cover by 1 to 2 in [2.5 to 5 cm]. Place the pot over high heat and bring to a boil. Lower the heat to a gentle simmer and cook, uncovered, for 1½ to 2 hours, or until tender. (It might be necessary to add more water to keep the beans covered as they cook.) Turn off the heat, stir in 1 tsp of salt, and let the beans cool in their cooking water for 20 minutes. Drain, saving the cooking water to add to soups.

On Butcher's Cuts

While Americans can go to a butcher's shop and ask for a rib-eye steak without any awareness of what part of the cow it comes from, Armenians describe cuts of meat based on an animal's anatomy. The best example of this is with Tjvjik (page 210), a dish of offal and onions so beloved that preparing it inspired a movie by the same name. Replicating the same cuts in America took a little detective work, but we found that lean cuts of meat, such as eye of round, work well for finely minced preparations, such as Chikufta (page 126), while more expensive cuts, like chops and loins, are the best for khorovats (Armenian grilling). Also, keep your eyes out for calves' feet to make Khash (page 156), a rich bone broth.

On Pantry Staples

APPLE CIDER VINEGAR Many of the sour and tangy flavors in Armenian cuisine come from tart herbs, such as sorrel, salt-brined pickles, or sour dried fruit, so vinegar is used sparingly. When it is used, it's most often apple cider vinegar. Choose unfiltered apple cider vinegar for a rounder, less acidic flavor.

> **A NOTE ON SALT:** Armenians are not shy about seasoning with salt, which may have evolved from centuries of using salt as a way to preserve food before refrigeration. The mineral represented life, and for this reason was stored in ceramic containers shaped like a pregnant woman. Still, everyone has a different idea of what tastes salty to them. All of the salt measurements used in this book were made with Diamond Crystal kosher salt because it is widely available in the United States. Feel free to use other salts, but be aware that some are saltier than others. Morton kosher salt and fine sea salts are about one-and-a-half times as

salty as Diamond Crystal by volume. Meanwhile, table salt is about twice as salty. If you are using a different kind of salt and are worried about making a dish too salty, reduce the salt by a quarter to a half. For everything but baking recipes, you can always add more at the end.

SPICES Syrian Armenians—many of whom came from Aleppo, a city famous for its eponymous dried peppers—are upping the quality and selection of spices in Yerevan. At Zeituna, a Western Armenian restaurant started by the Rastkelenians, a Syrian-Armenian family, cumin, ground dried peppers, and sumac (a tart ground red berry) season nearly everything. Yet to many Yerevantsis, these spices still taste exotic, and most home kitchens take a modest approach with seasoning. In Armenian home kitchens, black pepper and paprika season everything from vegetables to fish and meat. The paprika is mild and unsmoked; look for "sweet paprika" on the label. Smoked paprika is not a perfect substitute, especially in subtler recipes like Green Salad with Radishes (page 98). Other common spices in Armenia include juniper berries and bay leaves, which are used in pickling brines. Bay leaves play a minor role in stews.

If you like heat or generally are used to cooking with a lot of spices, consider adding a few pinches of ground or crushed dried peppers, such as Aleppo pepper, to the recipes in this book or offer some at the table. It's an especially good way to perk up stews such as Khashlama (page 208) and Chanakh (page 204). As of writing this book, the supply of Aleppo pepper is not actually coming from Aleppo, but pepper plant cultivars from the region are being grown elsewhere (mainly Turkey) and are still labeled as Aleppo. Marash pepper is similar, and both ground peppers are imported by companies such as Kalustyan's.

SUNFLOWER OIL On the grounds of Tatev Monastery in southern Armenia sits a small room with an enormous stone mill once used to grind sesame seeds into oil. In Armenia today, seed oils still prevail, though these days sunflower seed oil is the most common, as it is in other former Soviet republics. The best-quality sunflower seed oils are made by brands such as Spectrum and La Tourangelle, though a good alternative is grapeseed oil. Olive oil sold in Armenia tends to be expensive and of mixed quality, and therefore isn't used often. If you choose to use it while cooking from this book, select a mild olive oil that won't impart too many herbal or grassy flavors to the finished dish. Olive oil is especially good to use on Chikufta (page 126) and Eech (page 129).

EXTRAS Red pepper paste is most often used in Western Armenian–style dishes, like lahmajo, but you can also add red pepper paste in recipes that use tomato paste if you desire a bit of pepper flavor. Look for red pepper paste at Middle Eastern and Russian markets, and taste it before adding it to your food to check its salt and spice levels. Pomegranate molasses (*doshab* means any kind of fruit molasses, including pomegranate) is used sparingly, though a drop mixed into a salad dressing or meat marinade can do wonders for rounding out flavors as well as increasing

caramelization. In this book, grape molasses is used in Sweet Soujuk (page 229); it is made by dipping strands of walnuts in thickened grape juice. Molasses is also made from mulberries in Armenia, though it is hard to find in America.

On Measurements and Cookware

Cooking in Armenia relies more on the eye than the measuring cup. To re-create the recipes in the United States, however, we needed to be more precise. The recipes in this book include both American measurements and metric equivalents. In many cases, the metric equivalent is rounded up or down to make it easier to follow, as when describing the size of a pot or pan. If you don't have the exact-size pan called for when making a stew or soup, work with what you typically use for similar recipes.

On Herbs

When we visited the lavash bakery in Argel, Ara's eyes lit up when he thought he had spotted a large jar of pickled ramps in front of a neighbor's house. They sold him the jar, he dug in, and that's when confusion set in. What were those bitter things? Later we found out the so-called ramp was *sindrick*, which is picked in the spring and pickled or served boiled with vinegar. This was not the first time we encountered a green that was completely new to us, with good reason: More than a quarter of the plants that grow in Armenia are *only* grown in Armenia. The country's rich biodiversity is one of the reasons that a range of wild herbs, such as purslane, goosefoot, and several kinds of sorrel, plays such a role in its cooking. If you happen upon a trove of edible wild greens, make use of them in recipes such as Jingalov Hats (page 58), Greens with Eggs (page 122), or any of the soups.

Armenian cooks go light on spice but generous on fresh herbs, so unless dried herbs are called for in this book, assume all herbs in recipes are fresh. Markets sell bouquets of mixed herbs—*khar' kanachi*—containing flat-leaf parsley, cilantro, dill, and opal basil, and sometimes even chervil and tarragon. When cooking from this book, go with bright-looking herbs with tender stems whenever possible. If herbs like opal (purple) basil are hard to find, stick with cilantro, parsley, and dill. (Some grocery stores will order opal basil if you call in advance.) Cilantro and parsley can be washed, dried with a salad spinner, and then stored in zip-top plastic bags for up to 1 week. Dill, chervil, tarragon, and basil are best eaten a day or two after being washed. If the herbs look a bit tired, snip off 1 in [2.5 cm] of their stems and set them in a glass of water to perk them up. For a deeper dive into Armenian herbs, see Jingalov Hats Herbs and Greens (page 63).

CHOPPING HERBS Unless the stems are quite tough, which can be the case for tarragon, parsley, and dill, use the stems and leaves when cooking with herbs. Armenians have an efficient technique for chopping bunches of herbs that yields a perfect mix of stems and leaves: Gather a bunch of herbs in one hand. Slice the bunch in half so the ends are separated from the tops. Next, put the two cut ends together to form a bundle with one neat edge and slice through them finely.

DRIED HERBS Used more often for tea than for seasoning food, dried herbs are nevertheless an important part of the Armenian pantry. The two most notable are *aveluk*, a wild, sour herb often called sorrel (though it is a much longer leaf than French sorrel), and *urtz*, a kind of thyme. Urtz is the word for both dried thyme and the tea made with it, yet urtz as a tea also often contains summer savory.

Herb and Cheese Plate

Alongside a basket of bread, every single meal in Armenia—whether it's breakfast, lunch, or dinner—includes a plate of herbs and cheese. You help yourself to lavash and then wrap sprigs of herbs and greens, such as radish greens or skinny green onions, and salty cheese—or whatever you want—inside it. Replicate the experience by selecting at least two fresh herbs and a salty cheese, such as feta, and then some green onions and radishes with their leaves, if you have them. For more variety, add sliced Persian cucumbers, sliced tomatoes, and Salt-Brined Mixed Pickles (page 134). The same mixed herbs left over from an herb and cheese plate can be chopped and sprinkled on top of just about all the soups and stews in this book.

Baking from This Book

raditional Armenian baking is based on simple techniques using tools that are readily available. To stay true to their spirit, our baking recipes are low-tech and meant to look like they were made by hand. Like many types of baking, mastery comes with repetition, and the second or third batch of lavash or *matnakash* is bound to be a little easier than the first. The descriptions that follow explain why we use a certain tool, what we mean when we say "lukewarm water," and how we prefer to measure flour. Before baking any of the flatbreads, be sure to review Heat Sources (page 40).

Equipment and Tools

KITCHEN SCALE This is the most accurate and easiest way to portion flour and other ingredients, allowing you to weigh everything in one bowl. If you prefer measuring cups, portion by the "scoop and level" method, dipping the cup into the flour, dragging it through until full, and then leveling it off. One cup of flour will be about 140 g.

OTHER MEASURING DEVICES For smaller quantities, teaspoons and tablespoons are usually more accurate than kitchen scales. A small liquid measuring cup that ranges from 1 Tbsp [15 ml] to ¼ cup [60 ml] is handy for measuring oils and other liquid ingredients in small amounts.

PLASTIC DOUGH SCRAPER This inexpensive, flexible tool makes it easy to remove dough from a bowl, scrape sticky dough off the counter, and cut and portion dough. It's also handy when mixing dough for pastries, such as Gata (page 235).

ROLLING PIN A sturdy American (with handles) or French (no handles, with either straight or tapered ends) rolling pin works well for rolling out doughs in this book. Usually the heavier the rolling pin, the better. To cut the noodles for Arishta (page 76), some like to use a special grooved, heavy rolling pin.

STAND MIXER For the most hands-off bread-making experience, use a stand mixer with the paddle and dough hook attachments to make easy work of mixing and kneading. (Its whisk attachment comes in handy when making desserts, like Goris Baklava, page 239.) It's not essential to own a stand mixer to bake from this book because recipes also have instructions for kneading by hand.

HALF-SHEET PANS Rimmed 13 by 18 in [23 by 33 cm] baking pans are easily one of the most useful pans to have in any kitchen. Line them with towels for drying herbs, flip them over to make a makeshift pizza peel, turn them into a baking surface in place of a baking stone, and use them right-side up for roasting or baking just about anything.

PIZZA PEEL A pizza peel resembles an oversize ping-pong paddle, and the shape makes it easy to move flatbread in and out of the oven when baking on a pizza stone. You can create the same effect using a rimless cutting board, an overturned half-sheet pan, or anything that will help you slide dough onto a hot oven surface in one quick motion.

PARCHMENT PAPER Flatbreads with toppings, such as Lahmajo (page 64), are easier to transfer to the oven if you shape and bake them directly on parchment paper. Shape the dough on a sheet of parchment paper, add the toppings, and then slide the parchment paper directly onto the pizza stone in the oven. The paper will turn brown with the oven's heat, but the cooking process is over before the paper burns.

Buying parchment paper precut to fit inside a half-sheet pan makes using it so much easier. Look for precut parchment paper at restaurant supply stores or online at King Arthur (kingarthurflour.com).

A FEW THOUGHTS ABOUT PLASTIC WRAP
As dough rises, it needs to be covered to avoid drying out. Plastic wrap is one option, but there are others to consider. In Armenia, where people still work in the waste-not-want-not ethos of Soviet times, we saw bakers cover dough with kitchen towels and home cooks cut plastic bags into squares to reuse. All this is to say that it is possible to reduce plastic wrap use and bake great bread. Here are a few options:

- Invest in an 8 cup [2 L] glass measuring cup that comes with a lid. (Pyrex makes one.) After kneading, place the dough in the measuring cup, cover it, and note its height on the glass with a piece of tape. This will make it easier to see when the dough has doubled in volume.

- While the dough rests at room temperature, cover it with a floured kitchen towel or linen napkin (avoid terry cloth because it sticks to dough). If a skin forms on the dough, spritz it with water from a spray bottle to rehydrate it.

- Other workarounds include experimenting with silicone lids, beeswax wrap, and other reusable covers. If plastic wrap is the best option, coat it lightly with oil on the side facing the dough so the plastic won't stick to the dough when it rises.

Baking Ingredients

FLOUR After working with a variety of combinations, we discovered that you can be flexible with flour choice when baking flatbreads, as long as you're using wheat flours and not gluten-free varieties. To keep things simple, you can also stick with all-purpose flour when baking from this book.

HERITAGE FLOURS If you are interested in locally milled grains, mix some into the recipe in place of a portion of the all-purpose flour. If it's a deeper-colored, hearty whole wheat flour, like Turkey Red, start by substituting it for a quarter of the all-purpose flour and monitor the results. If it's a lighter style of wheat, like Sonora or Red Fife, you can use it interchangeably with the all-purpose flour for the flatbreads in this book. You can also experiment with substituting up to a quarter of the all-purpose flour for whole wheat flour in sweeter recipes, such as Gata (page 235).

Heritage grain expert Ellen King of Hewn Bakery in Evanston, Illinois, says moisture levels of heritage flours change with the season. If a dough feels dry, she dips her hands into water and gently kneads the dough. She then lets it rest for several minutes to absorb the water.

Buy whole wheat flours in smaller quantities and freeze them if not using right away to prevent them from going rancid.

WATER "Lukewarm" in these recipes indicates water that is comfortable to touch, feeling slightly warmer than your fingers but not hot. If it is hot in the kitchen, opt for cooler water, about 75°F [24°C]. If your kitchen is cold, use warmer water, but no hotter than 100°F [38°C].

YEAST For the recipes in this book that use yeast, choose instant yeast; it is more concentrated and has a longer shelf life than active dry yeast. Depending on the brand, it is also called fast-rising yeast, quick-rising yeast, bread machine yeast, or RapidRise (but it doesn't make dough rise faster). Store opened packets of yeast for up to 4 months in the refrigerator or 6 months in the freezer to keep them fresh.

SALT Like the other recipes in this book, the salt used to develop the bread recipes is Diamond Crystal kosher salt. If you prefer baking with fine sea salt, reduce the quantity by 25 percent. (See page 33 for more on salt.)

SUGAR The sugar used in Armenia most closely resembles organic cane sugar in that it looks slightly less refined than granulated sugar in the United States. Still, the difference between the two is negligible for the recipes in this book, and either can be used.

Baking Tips

Most breads require these main steps: making the dough, letting it rest after kneading (the primary fermentation), portioning the dough and letting it rest again (the secondary fermentation, or proofing stage), and then baking the dough, or, in the case of some flatbreads, griddling it. While most of the steps are explained in the recipes, here are a few more pointers.

OLD DOUGH In baker terminology, this is called a "preferment": a mix of flour, water, and yeast that is made before the main dough and can boost the flavor and structure of bread. In this book, we use old dough to make Lavash (page 48) and Matnakash (page 68) to give the dough more flavor and make it easier to shape. When making lavash dough, you can save one ball from a batch and use it next time in place of the old dough. Covered and refrigerated, old dough keeps for about 3 days. An oiled 2 cup [480 ml] resealable container is a good storage vessel.

KNEADING AND RESTING A key step in mixing and kneading bread dough is letting the dough rest right after combining the flour, water, and old dough. The technical term for this step is *autolyse*, a brief pause that allows the flour to absorb the water and for gluten strands to begin forming. Resting the dough for 20 minutes in between kneading shortens the amount of time you need to spend actively kneading the dough.

PORTIONING AND SHAPING A kitchen scale is handy for dividing dough into equal-size pieces, but you can come close by first dividing the dough in half with a dough scraper, then in half again and again until you have the number of pieces needed. For the next step, shape the portions into balls by cupping your hand over each piece on the counter and moving it in a circle. If there is too much flour on the counter and there isn't enough friction between your hand and the dough to turn it into a ball, sprinkle a little water over the counter and try again.

ROLLING AND STRETCHING Once the dough has rested and relaxed after portioning, it's ready to be rolled out. The way to reach the right thinness is to first roll it using a rolling pin and then stretch it with your hands. Use only a small amount of flour on the counter for rolling; the dough is not sticky and a little friction can help it stretch. If the dough resists stretching, let it rest and start on another piece of dough.

Time

You can make flatbread recipes work for your schedule by refrigerating dough for a few days. Here are some options:

- **Make the old dough a few hours before mixing the main dough, or make the old dough the day before and refrigerate it. Let it come to room temperature for at least 2 hours before proceeding.**

- **Mix the main dough and let it rest for a few hours on the counter or overnight in the refrigerator.**

- **Portion the dough and let it rest for a third time. It can then be rolled out and cooked or baked within an hour or refrigerated one final time. Before rolling out the dough, bring it to room temperature for at least 2 hours if previously refrigerated. This works best for lavash; you can refrigerate portioned dough, allowing you to griddle half a batch one day and the remaining dough the next.**

Heat Sources for Baking or Griddling Flatbread

Here are a few options for achieving blistered, delicious flatbreads at home. For Lavash (page 48) and Jingalov Hats (page 58), using a hot surface on the stove allows the dough to puff and brown before it turns into a cracker. For other recipes, such as Lahmajo (page 64), Matnakash (page 68), and Tonir Hats (page 73), the oven works better because it evenly distributes heat. Still, everyone's kitchen is different; we've outlined the following options so you can choose what works best for you.

WOK An overturned carbon-steel wok resembles a makeshift *saj*, the type of griddle used for flatbreads throughout the Middle East, and it consistently made the best lavash in our tests. The wok works best with a gas burner, so skip this option if you have an electric stove. Be sure to use a seasoned carbon-steel wok—for instructions on how to season a wok, look to expert online advice, such as that from The Wok Shop in San Francisco (wokshop.com). Do not use a nonstick wok. If the wok has a metal handle, keep the counter and your hands safe by wrapping the handle with a towel.

To griddle, drape the stretched (or shaped) dough over the hot wok. If it folds over itself, pull it apart. You can drape lavash dough over a rolling pin to transfer it to the wok if it's easier.

BEST FOR: Lavash (page 48), Jingalov Hats (page 58)

CAST-IRON GRIDDLE Close to the wok in lavash-cooking performance, a cast-iron griddle runs 20 in [50 cm] long and covers two burners. If you don't have a griddle, you can also use a round cast-iron skillet: Follow the instructions for the cast-iron griddle, but instead of rolling out a full portion of lavash dough, divide the dough in half and roll it into a round to make smaller lavash. If you have an electric griddle, you can also use it for griddling flatbreads. It may not get quite as hot as the versions on a stove and will likely take longer to cook. In this case, use the visual cues in the recipes to tell when the flatbread is done.

BEST FOR: Lavash (page 48), Jingalov Hats (page 58)

GRILL Grilling lavash produces beautiful blisters on the bread. If you're using the grill for other things, you may want to grill lavash as well. (The lavash only takes seconds to cook, so it isn't practical to fire up a charcoal grill solely for the purpose of lavash.) Unlike Armenian-style barbecue setups (see page 162), you will need a standard grill with grates. Be sure to clean the grates well with a grill brush and oil them before you start grilling to prevent the dough from sticking. Have a half-sheet pan lightly coated in oil handy for transporting rolled-out dough from the counter to the grill and a pair of tongs to pick up the lavash off the grill.

BEST FOR: Lavash (page 48)

BAKING STONE OR BAKING STEEL

Baking flatbreads in an oven with a preheated stone or steel allows the bread to achieve a crisp crust. While it tends to dry out lavash, it is great for lavash dough with toppings, like lahmajo, and thicker kinds of flatbread, like matnakash and tonir hats. If you don't have a baking stone, you can create a makeshift one out of an overturned half-sheet pan. Just place the pan in the oven upside down 5 minutes before baking.

BEST FOR: Lahmajo (page 64),
Matnakash (page 68),
Tonir Hats (page 73)

Buying Lavash

When buying lavash, look for very thin bread that comes folded in bundles at Armenian or Middle Eastern stores. It should be no thicker than a crepe and have a few blisters, with a texture that is pliable and easy to fold. To keep it from drying out, store the lavash in sealed plastic bags. Purchased lavash is perfect for making Lavash-Wrapped Trout (page 183), Lavash-Wrapped Etchmiadzin Kufta (page 189), or Bean Lavash Triangles (page 117). In general, purchased lavash sheets will be longer and wider than homemade lavash; one purchased sheet is the equivalent of two or three homemade sheets.

Around the Tonir

Flatbreads and Noodles

read—*hats*—is the foundation of every meal in Armenia. Even saying "let's eat" (*hats untenk*), translates to "let's eat bread." If you're a good host, you are someone who "eats bread." And if you're an ungrateful person, you are "without bread or salt."

It's likely that bread has been made in Armenia since prehistoric times. In 2018, archaeologists discovered bread crumbs in a firepit in Jordan that date back more than 14,000 years, predating the advent of agriculture. Instead of farming preceding baking, hunter-gatherers may have started planting wild wheat because bread was so valuable to them. Either way, evidence of wheat cultivation in the Ararat Valley, Armenia's agricultural heartland, dates back to the Neolithic period. The primordial act of grinding wheat berries to make flour, kneading a dough, and baking it on the walls of a clay firepit continues today with lavash.

Eating lavash fresh from the tonir is as good as it gets, but it's also possible to make it at home with satisfying results. When we started our research, however, we weren't so sure; was this going to be one of those things like New York City bagels or San Francisco sourdough—where location (the water, the air, the who-knows-what) was crucial for success? Could we replicate lavash, as well as other breads we loved, outside of Armenia? The answer is yes, though it took some sleuthing and practice.

Our first question centered around yeast—did bakers use it to give the flatbread a bit more puff? In Yerevan, our first stop was GUM (pronounced "goom," an abbreviation of the Russian phrase "State Universal Store"), a large, mostly indoor marketplace where stacks of lavash line a row of stalls. The women selling lavash at GUM weren't bakers, but they confirmed that the lavash they sold contained *drozh* (a shortened version of the Russian word for yeast). But was it commercial yeast or something like a sourdough starter? We next drove to villages outside of Yerevan, talking to bakers in Yeghvard and Argel who confirmed that they not only used yeast but also held back some of the dough from a previous batch to mix into the next batch. This old dough—*ttkhmor* ("tut-kmore") in Armenian—gave the bread flavor and structure. In the old days, the only thing added was ttkhmor, but the women who bake lavash today prefer the consistency of adding a bit of yeast along with it.

The way the dough is mixed is also important. In the village of Argel, baker Lusine Abrahamyan lets the dough rest halfway through kneading it to make it smoother—a step bakers in the West call autolyse. They also are immensely practical, using warmer water to make dough when it's cold outside and cold water in the summer when it's hot. These tips would be easy to translate in

a recipe. It was a little trickier finding a way to bake lavash at home, but after a lot of tinkering with different heat sources and surfaces, we came away with blistered, chewy, pliable lavash.

Lavash is a jumping-off point for further exploration into the world of Armenian hats, which range from Lahmajo (page 64), the so-called "Armenian pizza" popular throughout the diaspora, to Jingalov Hats (page 58), a flatbread filled with herbs so prized in the Republic of Artsakh (see page 85) that no trip there is complete without eating it.

While some of the recipes in this chapter have unique doughs, others have crossovers. The Lavash (page 48) and Whole Wheat Lavash recipe (page 54) can also be used as the base for lahmajo, while the Matnakash recipe (page 68), shaped in a different way, turns into Tonir Hats (page 73), another flatbread from Artsakh.

The chapter ends with Armenian-style noodles, highlighting a few other ways in which Armenians leverage the combination of flour and water to make something greater than the sum of its parts.

Before starting the recipes in this chapter, review Baking from This Book, page 36.

Lavash

Լավաշ

This lavash recipe takes what we learned from Armenia's master lavash bakers and adapts it to the realities of a modern home kitchen. It makes a forgiving dough that can bend to your schedule: You can make the first step—the old dough—and the final product in about 6 hours, or you can spread the work out over the course of a couple days. The instructions that follow include options for cooking lavash on a wok, cast-iron griddle, or grill. Before starting, review Baking from This Book (page 36) to sort out the heat source that works best for you. The less time the lavash spends cooking, the more pliable it will be. If the lavash griddles up into a crisp cracker, that's okay too; spritz it with water, cover it in a towel, and it should soften.

Griddling the first lavash is like cooking the first pancake in the batch, and you may have to adjust the heat of the cooking surface to prevent parts of it from burning before the rest is cooked. That's okay; in Armenia, there's a saying attributed to the poet Paruyr Sevak that the first lavash baked in the fire is like a first love—it's too hot to last. "Whatever you do, it will fall off the wall of the tonir and burn away," he wrote. Here we're hoping to instill a slow-burning, long-lasting kind of lavash love.

-continued

Makes eight 13 by 9 in
[33 by 23 cm] sheets

OLD DOUGH

½ cup [70 g] all-purpose flour

¼ cup plus a scant 1 Tbsp [70 ml] lukewarm water (see page 38)

¼ tsp instant yeast

DOUGH

1 cup [240 ml] lukewarm water (see page 38)

1 Tbsp sunflower oil or other neutral oil

2 tsp kosher salt

3 cups plus 2 Tbsp [440 g] all-purpose flour, plus more for dusting

To make the old dough, using your hands or a rubber spatula, squish together the flour, water, and yeast in a bowl until it forms a thick paste. Scrape the paste into a small, lightly oiled container, cover, and let it sit out for 1½ to 2 hours, or refrigerate overnight and bring to room temperature for at least 2 hours before using. When ready, the ball will have doubled in volume.

To make the dough, in the bowl of a stand mixer, combine the old dough, water, oil, and salt. Squish the old dough with your hands to break it up in the water; it doesn't have to be perfectly mixed in.

Fit the stand mixer with the paddle attachment and add a third of the flour. Mix on low speed until the dough looks like pancake batter. Add the remaining flour and mix on low speed until incorporated. Remove the paddle attachment, pulling off any dough stuck to it. If there is flour

at the base of the bowl, use your hands to press the dough into the flour. Cover the bowl with a kitchen towel and let the dough sit for 20 minutes to allow the flour to hydrate.

(To make by hand, combine the old dough, water, oil, and salt in a large bowl and mix together, squishing the old dough into the water with your hands. Stir in the flour gradually with your fingers until a crumbly dough forms, then knead it a few times in the bowl by folding the dough over itself and pressing it down into the bowl. Cover the bowl with a kitchen towel and let the dough rest for 20 minutes.)

Remove the towel and attach the dough hook to the stand mixer. Mix the dough on medium speed until the dough releases from the sides of the bowl without sticking and feels smooth to the touch, about 4 minutes. Turn the mixer off and reposition the dough to the center of the bowl if it seems to get stuck on one side of the bowl.

(To knead by hand, dust the counter lightly with flour and place the dough on top. Begin kneading by stretching and folding the dough over itself until it is smooth to the touch, 5 to 7 minutes.)

Lightly oil an 8 cup [2 L] glass Pyrex or a large glass bowl and place the dough inside. Cover the bowl with a lid, a plate, or plastic wrap, and let it rest for 3 hours or until doubled in volume. Or refrigerate overnight and let the dough come to room temperature for at least 2 hours before portioning.

-continued

To portion and shape the dough, dust the counter lightly with flour and place the dough on top. Using a bench scraper or knife, cut the dough into eight pieces about 3.5 oz [100 g] each.

To shape the dough, cup the palm of your hand over one portion at a time and move your hand in a circle. The friction from the counter will help form the dough into a ball. If there is too much flour on the surface and the dough is sliding around, give the counter a spritz of water and try again. Lightly oil a rimmed tray and place the dough on the tray, ensuring that the portions are not touching. Cover with a kitchen towel or plastic wrap lightly coated with oil. Leave out for 1 to 1½ hours, or until puffy, or refrigerate for up to 3 days. If you refrigerate the dough, use plastic wrap to cover it and expect it to take an hour or two to return to room temperature before it is ready to be rolled out.

Dust the counter lightly with flour. Pat a portion of dough into an oval with your fingertips. Using a rolling pin and moving back and forth, roll the dough as thinly as possible into an oval about 13 by 9 in [33 by 23 cm]. If the dough resists stretching, let it relax and start working on another portion before returning to it. You can also gently stretch the dough with your hands to correct the shape. It doesn't have to look perfect. To griddle the lavash, follow the instuctions on the facing page.

NOTE: To turn leftover lavash into crackers, tear or cut the lavash into chip-size pieces and place them in a single layer on a sheet pan. Brush the pieces with a little oil, sprinkle them with salt, and then toast them at 400°F [200°C] until golden brown and crispy, about 6 minutes.

To griddle lavash, choose one of the following options:

OVERTURNED WOK Place a carbon-steel wok upside down over a burner. Have a pair of tongs handy.

Heat the wok over high heat for 1 minute or until a sprinkle of water instantly evaporates.

Drape the dough over the wok. Cook for 1 minute or until you can lift it easily from the wok with tongs and it has puffed slightly and blistered. Turn the dough over to briefly cook the other side, no more than 30 seconds. For extra browning, flip it over for another 30 seconds.

Transfer the lavash to a half-sheet pan and cover with a dry kitchen towel while you cook the rest of the dough. In between batches, turn off the burner. The wok heats up quickly, and it will get too hot if the burner is left on.

CAST-IRON GRIDDLE Place a 20 in [50 cm] cast-iron griddle over two burners. Heat the griddle over medium-high heat for a few minutes or until a sprinkle of water instantly evaporates.

Drape the dough over the griddle. Cook for 1 minute or until you can lift the dough easily with tongs and it has puffed slightly and blistered. Turn the dough over to briefly cook the other side, no more than 30 seconds. For extra browning, flip it over for 30 more seconds.

Transfer the lavash to a half-sheet pan and cover with a dry kitchen towel while you cook the rest of the dough. In between batches, keep the griddle turned on, but monitor its heat so it doesn't get too hot.

GRILL Have tongs, a pastry brush, a small bowl of vegetable oil, and 2 half-sheet pans ready. Coat one of the pans lightly with oil.

Heat a gas grill over medium-high heat or prepare a charcoal grill for direct-heat cooking. Ensure that the grill grates are clean. The grill should be hot enough that you can only hold your hand over the grates for 3 to 5 seconds. Place a sheet of dough onto the oiled pan and brush oil on top. Drape the oiled dough over the grill. Cover the grill and cook for 25 seconds. Uncover the grill. Using tongs, turn the lavash over and let it cook for another 25 seconds, uncovered, or until evenly blistered and puffed in parts.

Transfer to the clean half-sheet pan and cover with a dry kitchen towel while you cook the rest of the dough.

Eat the lavash soon after making it or store it in plastic bags to keep the bread pliable. It's okay if it dries out and turns brittle; just rehydrate it by misting the lavash with water and covering it with a towel to let it soften. Soon after, it should be pliable enough to roll up without cracking. If it's still cracking, mist with more water.

Whole Wheat Lavash

Լավաշ գործենի ամբողջահատիկից

Whole-grain wheat flours used to be much more common in the days when Armenian villages shared a mill, grinding the wheat of different families together. Exactly what kind of wheat they milled isn't clear, but it was likely a mix of winter and spring wheat and, in lean years, other grains not typically used in making bread. Now nearly everyone uses the same white, all-purpose wheat flour.

At Crumbs in Yerevan, Ani Harutyunyan is trying to bring whole-grain flours back into baking. Her hope is that more people in Armenia's capital city will follow her lead and reclaim Armenia's whole-grain heritage. While Ani doesn't make lavash at Crumbs, she shared her whole wheat recipe with us, which we adapted here. Melted butter draws out the nutty flavors of the flour, but oil can be used in its place if you'd prefer to keep the lavash free of dairy.

-continued

Makes eight 13 by 9 in
[33 by 23 cm] sheets

OLD DOUGH

½ cup [70 g] whole wheat flour

¼ cup plus 2 Tbsp [90 ml] lukewarm water (see page 38)

¼ tsp instant yeast

DOUGH

1¼ cups [300 ml] lukewarm water (see page 38)

1 Tbsp butter, melted

2 tsp kosher salt

1 cup [140 g] whole wheat flour

2¼ cups [315 g] all-purpose flour, plus more for dusting

To make the old dough, using your hands or a rubber spatula, squish together the flour, water, and yeast in a bowl until it forms a thick paste. Scrape the paste into a small, lightly oiled container, cover, and let it sit out for 1½ to 2 hours, or refrigerate for up to 3 days and bring to room temperature for at least 2 hours before using. The ball will not have changed much compared with old dough made with all-purpose flour for the lavash recipe on page 48, but it will smell yeasty and will have puffed up a little.

To make the dough, in the bowl of a stand mixer, combine the old dough, water, butter, and salt. Squish the old dough with your hands to break it up in the water; it doesn't have to be perfectly mixed in.

Fit the stand mixer with the paddle attachment and add the whole wheat flour. Mix on low speed until the dough looks like pancake batter.

Add the all-purpose flour and mix on low until incorporated. Remove the paddle attachment, pulling off any dough stuck to it. If there is flour at the base of the bowl, use your hands to press the dough into the flour. Cover the bowl with a kitchen towel and let the dough sit for 20 minutes to allow the flour to hydrate.

(To make by hand, combine the old dough, water, butter, and salt in a large bowl and mix together, squishing the old dough into the water with your hands. Stir in the flours gradually with your fingers until a coarse dough forms, then knead it a few times in the bowl by folding the dough over itself and pressing it down into the bowl. Cover the bowl with a kitchen towel and let the dough rest for 20 minutes.)

Remove the towel and attach the dough hook to the stand mixer. Mix the dough on medium speed until the dough releases from the sides of the bowl without sticking and feels smooth to the touch, about 4 minutes. Turn the mixer off and reposition the dough to the center of the bowl if it seems to get stuck on one side of the bowl.

(To knead by hand, dust the counter lightly with flour and place the dough on top. Begin kneading by stretching and folding the dough over itself until it is smooth to the touch, 5 to 7 minutes.)

Lightly oil an 8 cup [2 L] glass Pyrex or large glass bowl and place the dough inside. Cover the bowl with a lid, a plate, or plastic wrap, and let it rest for 3 hours or until nearly doubled in volume. Or refrigerate overnight and let the

dough come to room temperature for at least 2 hours before portioning.

To portion and shape the dough, dust the counter lightly with flour and place the dough on top. Using a bench scraper or knife, cut the dough into eight pieces about 3.8 oz [110 g] each.

To shape the dough, cup the palm of your hand over one portion at a time and move your hand in a circle. The friction from the counter will help form the dough into a ball. If there is too much flour on the surface and the dough is sliding around, give the counter a spritz of water and try again. Lightly oil a rimmed tray and place the dough on the tray, ensuring that the portions are not touching. Cover with a kitchen towel or plastic wrap lightly coated with oil. Leave out for 1 to 1½ hours or until puffy, or refrigerate for up

to 3 days. If you refrigerate the dough, use plastic wrap to cover it and expect it to take an hour or two to return to room temperature before it is ready to be rolled out.

Dust the counter lightly with flour. Pat a portion of dough into a rectangle with your fingertips. Using a rolling pin and moving back and forth, roll the dough as thinly as possible into an oval about 13 by 9 in [33 by 23 cm]. If the dough resists stretching, let it relax and start working on another portion before returning to it. You can also gently stretch it with your hands to correct the shape. It doesn't have to look perfect. To griddle the lavash, follow the instructions on page 53.

Jingalov Hats

ժ ի ն գ յ ա լ ո վ հ ա ց

flatbreads filled with greens

"Did you eat *jingalov hats*?" That's the first question anyone in Yerevan asked us when we said we had visited Artsakh (page 85). If they had known earlier, they may have asked us to bring back a box of these beloved flatbreads from the bazaar in Stepanakert, the small republic's capital city.

These breads—*hats* in Armenian—look like flat footballs and are filled to the brim with herbs and greens. Some bakers claim they use more than twenty types of greens to achieve optimal flavor. This is easier in the spring, when foraged herbs—some of them rarely seen outside of Armenia—pad the numbers. By November, the number dwindles to "merely" a dozen herbs and greens. To get the best mix from what's available near you, see Jingalov Hats Herbs and Greens (page 63).

-continued

Makes four 8 in [20 cm] hats

When making jingalov hats, mix the dough first and let it rest while you finely chop all of the greens and herbs. It's best to wash the greens the day before or earlier the day of so they are dry when you are ready to chop them, making it easier to slice them as thinly as possible (this helps them cook quickly inside the flatbread as you griddle it). By the time you're done chopping, the dough will be ready to portion. For cooking the hats, Artsakh cooks prefer a cast-iron saj, but a large griddle that covers two burners works just as well. If you have extra dough from making Lavash (page 48), you can use it in place of the dough called for here for a slightly puffier version. And if you run out of greens, roll out the extra dough and griddle it as if it were lavash.

DOUGH

⅔ cup [160 ml] lukewarm water (see page 38)

1 tsp kosher salt

1½ cups [210 g] all-purpose flour, plus more for dusting

FILLING

8 heaping cups [440 g] finely sliced greens and herbs (see Jingalov Hats Herbs and Greens, page 63), such as:

> 4 cups [220 g] neutral greens
>
> 2 cups [110 g] herbal herbs
>
> 2 cups [110 g] sour greens and herbs

3 green onions, thinly sliced

2 tsp sweet paprika

1 tsp kosher salt

½ tsp red pepper flakes

1½ Tbsp sunflower oil or other neutral oil

1 Tbsp lemon juice

Handful of pomegranate seeds (optional)

To make the dough, in a large bowl, combine the water and salt. Add the flour gradually with your hands to incorporate. Knead briefly in the bowl. (It's okay if it's slightly sticky at this point.)

Dust the counter with flour. Turn the dough out onto the counter and knead until it is just starting to become smooth, about 4 minutes. Roll the dough into a ball, place it in a lightly oiled bowl, cover with a kitchen towel, and let it rest while you chop the greens and herbs. It will soften and become smoother as it rests.

After at least 20 minutes (or up to an hour), place the dough on the floured counter and divide it into four equal pieces, about 3 oz [85 g] each. To shape the dough, cup the palm of your hand over one portion at a time and move your hand in a circle. The friction from the counter will help form the dough into a ball. If there is too much flour on the surface and the dough is sliding around, give the counter a spritz of water and try again.

To make the filling, mix the greens with the green onions, paprika, salt, red pepper flakes, oil, and lemon juice, mixing well with your hands to ensure everything is seasoned.

To shape the jingalov hats, lightly dust the counter with flour. Pat a ball of dough into a round. Using a rolling pin, roll the dough into a thin circle about 8 in [20 cm] in diameter.

Place about 2 cups [110 g] of the filling in the center of the dough circle. Sprinkle with pomegranate seeds, if using. Pick up two sides of the circle and pinch them together over the center of the filling, almost like sealing pie crust. (See page 62 for the step-by-step sequence.) Continue to pinch the edges together from top to bottom so that the middle is wide and the ends form points. When you get to the end, tuck in the tip so it's sealed but ensure that there is filling all the way to the tip.

Firmly press the seam with the edge of your hand to ensure the dough is sealed. Turn over and flatten the dough with the palm of your hand so that it resembles a deflated football. It should be ¼ to ½ in [6 to 12 mm] thick. If thicker, roll with a rolling pin to flatten.

To cook the jingalov hats, heat a 20 in [50 cm] cast-iron griddle or pan over medium-high heat. Place the filled dough, seam-side down, in the center. Lower the heat to medium and cook for 2½ to 3 minutes, until it is evenly brown. Flip over and continue to cook on the remaining side for another 2 minutes. If the dough still seems a little pale or raw, adjust the heat to medium-high and continue to cook the flatbread, flipping it over now and again so it cooks evenly. While the first flatbread cooks, start rolling out and filling the dough for the second jingalov hats.

Using a spatula, transfer the cooked flatbread to a serving platter and repeat the process with the remaining dough and filling.

Serve warm or at room temperature. Alternatively, cool completely and freeze for up to 2 months. Jingalov hats can be reheated by popping them in the oven at 400°F [200°C] for about 10 minutes, or until hot and crispy on the edges. Otherwise, extra jingalov hats keep for a day at room temperature or in the refrigerator for up to 3 days.

Jingalov Hats
Herbs and Greens

Old-timers in Artsakh grumble that each generation gets lazier, adding fewer greens to the jingalov hats, but the truth is that the number is less important than the balance achieved within the mix, according to Artsakh native Lilia Harutyunyan, who invited us to her home outside of Yerevan for a jingalov hats tutorial.

Sour and sharp herbs like sorrel balance the herbal ones, such as cilantro and chervil, she explained. Also, add just enough green onion so the flavor comes through but not so much that all you taste is onion. A good majority of the greens are neutral, able to carry the flavor of the stronger herbs. When there aren't as many sour herbs available, women who make jingalov hats in the Stepanakert bazaar cheat with a pinch of citric

acid. Some home cooks even mix chopped fruit leathers made of sour plums to deliver that sour tang. Here, we've turned to lemon juice for a similar effect. For her signature sweet-tart finish, Lilia also adds a handful of pomegranate seeds.

For the previous recipe, use a mix of greens and herbs from three categories: neutral or earthy, herbal, and sour. For the herbal category, ensure you have at least three herbs, such as dill, parsley, and cilantro (dill being arguably the most important herb in this category for striking the right flavor). For the other two categories, opt for at least two when creating your mix. If you're not sure where a green that isn't on this list fits in, taste it to assess how to categorize it.

NEUTRAL OR EARTHY

Slice thick stem ends separately and very thinly.

Beet greens

Chard

Collards

Purslane

Spinach

HERBAL

Slice herb stems with leaves, only removing stems if tough.

Chervil

Cilantro

Dill

Flat-leaf parsley

Tarragon

SOUR

When necessary, slice thick stem ends separately and very thinly.

Dandelion greens

Radish tops

Sorrel

Watercress

Lahmajo

լ ա h մ ա ջ ո

"Armenian pizza" topped with ground meat

A staple food of the Armenian diaspora, *lahmajo* is eaten everywhere from Lebanon to Fresno, California, where it goes by the nickname "Armenian pizza." Is it strictly Armenian? And is it pizza? Well, many countries claim it as their own, and it's not pizza in the traditional sense—it's topped with a mix of ground meat and tomatoes with spices, and there's no cheese. (Its name is also subject to change, morphing into *lahmajoon* or *lahmajun*, among other variations.) In Yerevan, where it's as common as pizza-by-the-slice is in New York, the biggest recent change is flavor: When Syrian Armenians began moving to Yerevan, they brought their version of lahmajo, which had more spices. Once people tried these spiced-up versions at spots like Lahmajun Gaidz, it was hard to go back to milder times. Pair lahmajo with Green Salad with Radishes (page 98) and you have a complete meal.

If you don't have a pizza stone for baking, follow the instructions for using an overturned half-sheet pan (page 41). If you'd rather only make 4 rounds of lahmajo, freeze the remaining filling for a future lahmajo baking session and use the rest of the dough to make *za'atar hats* (see the sidebar on page 67) or lavash.

-continued

Makes 8

1 recipe Lavash dough (page 48), plus flour, for dusting

TOPPING

One 14.5 oz [411 g] can whole plum tomatoes

1 Tbsp tomato paste or red pepper paste

½ yellow onion, coarsely chopped

½ cup [20 g] coarsely chopped flat-leaf parsley, including stems

4 garlic cloves, coarsely chopped

1 Tbsp sunflower oil or other neutral oil

1 Tbsp sweet paprika

1½ tsp kosher salt

½ tsp ground cumin

½ tsp red pepper flakes

1 lb [455 g] ground lamb or lean beef

Finely chopped mint leaves, for garnish (optional)

Lemon wedges, for serving

Follow the directions to make the lavash dough portions (see page 50), stopping right before griddling them. The dough takes about 6 hours to make, shape, and proof, or you can spread the work out over the course of a couple of days by refrigerating it at different stages. If the dough has been refrigerated, bring to room temperature for at least 2 hours beforehand.

Place a baking stone or baking steel in the center of the oven and preheat to 550°F [290°C] or as high as it will go. Set out a couple of

half-sheet pans or platters to place the finished lahmajo on.

To make the topping, in a food processor or blender, pulse together the tomatoes, tomato paste, onion, parsley, garlic, oil, paprika, salt, cumin, and red pepper flakes. Place the meat in a bowl and pour the contents of the food processor over it. Using your hands, squish the tomato mixture into the meat until evenly incorporated. You will have about 4 cups [960 ml] of filling.

To shape the lahmajo, lightly dust the counter with flour (the dough will not be that sticky). Place a ball of dough in the center and pat into a round. Using a rolling pin, roll the dough into a thin circle about 10 in [25 cm] in diameter.

Slide a sheet of parchment paper onto a pizza peel or a large cutting board and place the dough on top. Spread slightly less than ½ cup [120 ml] of the tomato-meat topping evenly over the surface of the dough.

To bake the lahmajo, in one quick motion, slide the parchment off the peel directly onto the pizza stone in the oven. Bake for 5 to 6 minutes, or until the edges are evenly browned and the meat is cooked through. While the first lahmajo bakes, start rolling out the dough for the second.

To take the lahmajo out of the oven, slide the parchment paper onto the pizza peel or use a pair of tongs to pull the lahmajo and parchment paper onto a cutting board. If the topping looks wet but the parchment paper is getting too brown, remove the parchment paper and return the lahmajo to the oven for 1 to 2 more minutes until the topping is dry. Repeat with the remaining dough and topping, evenly dividing the topping among the dough portions.

Before serving, top with mint, if using. Offer lemon wedges at the table for seasoning. Once baked, extra lahmajo freeze well for up to 2 months and can be reheated in the oven at 400°F [200°C] for about 8 minutes, or until hot and crispy on the edges.

Za'atar Hats

Before the war in Syria, the bakery business in Aleppo was dominated by Armenians. So when Gaidzak (Gaidz) Jabakhtchurian and his mother, Salpy Chilingirian, left Syria and repatriated to Armenia, they fell back on what they knew: Their family had been selling lahmajo for three generations in Aleppo. At Lahmajun Gaidz, a subterranean spot near Yerevan's Republic Square, Gaidz wields paper-thin flatbreads in and out of a blazing-hot gas-fired oven. Lahmajo is the most popular order, but he's branched out, offering za'atar hats, a bread spread with oil and savory za'atar seasoning, and a flatbread spread with a fiery red pepper paste, among other breads. "The local people, they just don't eat a lot of chile peppers," Gaidz explains. "But as Syrian Armenians, we care about spices, about peppers—it's our style." He and his mom agree that native Yerevantsi are getting more accustomed to spices, but only a little at a time. If the seasoning is too hot for some, a glass of tan, a savory yogurt drink, counters the burn.

You can make za'atar hats with the lavash dough. Follow the instructions on shaping and baking the dough for lahmajo, but instead of topping each round with the seasoned meat mixture, sprinkle it with a generous tablespoon of za'atar and drizzle with a tablespoon of sunflower oil. Finish with a pinch of salt, then bake as recommended for lahmajo. Leftover za'atar hats keeps in a plastic bag on the counter for 3 days or frozen for up to 2 months.

Matnakash

Մատնաքաշ

bread "drawn by fingers"

"If people can fly to space, making *matnakash* is not so difficult." That was the answer we got when we asked Ghegham Grigoryan, a baker in Gyumri, if it was hard to replicate the shape of this Armenian bread. Did we mention that the *Gyumretsi* (people of Gyumri) are famous for their wise-cracking ways?

In a small bakery on Gorki Street marked with a sign out front that said *Dak Hats* ("hot bread"), we watched Ghegham and co-worker Hasmik Bughdaryan make matnakash. Slightly thicker and lighter than focaccia, with lines running across the surface, matnakash translates to "drawn by fingers," and it's often served alongside lavash as a thicker, breadier option.

To create the signature shape, use your hands to press a grid into the center of the dough and then stretch the bread into an oval before loading it in the oven. In between the shaping steps, the bakers let the dough rest in a thick layer of wheat bran for several minutes, which keeps the base from sticking to the counter. "Take me to America and I'll teach you everything you need to know about matnakash," Ghegham said as we left the shop.

-continued

Makes 2

OLD DOUGH

1 cup [140 g] all-purpose flour

½ cup [120 ml] lukewarm water
(see page 38)

¼ tsp instant yeast

DOUGH

1 cup [240 ml] lukewarm water
(see page 38)

1 tsp instant yeast

3 cups plus 2 Tbsp [440 g]
all-purpose flour, plus more for
dusting

1 Tbsp kosher salt

SHAPING AND BAKING

Wheat bran or whole wheat flour,
for dusting

½ cup [70 g] all-purpose flour, plus
more for dusting

¾ cup [180 ml] water

To make the old dough, using your hands or a rubber spatula, squish together the flour, water, and yeast in a bowl until it forms a soft ball. Scrape the paste into a small, lightly oiled container, cover, and let it sit out for about 2 hours, or refrigerate overnight and bring to room temperature for at least 2 hours before using. When ready, the ball will have doubled in volume.

To make the dough, in the bowl of a stand mixer, combine the old dough and water. Squish the old dough with your hands to break it up in the water.

Fit the mixer with the paddle attachment and add the yeast and a third of the flour. Mix on low speed until the dough looks like pancake batter. Add the remaining flour and mix on low speed until fully incorporated. Remove the paddle attachment, pulling off any dough stuck to it. Cover the bowl with a kitchen towel, and let it sit for 20 minutes to allow the flour to hydrate.

(To make by hand, combine the old dough and water in a large bowl and mix together, squishing the old dough into the water with your hands. Stir in the yeast and flour with your fingers until a crumbly dough forms and then knead it a few times in the bowl by folding the dough over itself and pressing it down into the bowl. Cover the bowl with a kitchen towel and let the dough rest for 20 minutes.)

Remove the towel and attach the dough hook to the mixer. Sprinkle the salt on top. Mix the dough on medium speed until it releases from the sides of the bowl without sticking, about 4 minutes. (It may seem sticky at first, but the salt will help the dough firm up.) It's okay if it sticks to the base of the bowl as long as it lifts cleanly off the sides.

(To knead by hand, dust the counter lightly with flour and place the dough on top. Sprinkle the top of the dough with the salt and knead, stretching and folding the dough over itself until it is smooth to the touch, 5 to 7 minutes.)

Lightly oil an 8 cup [2 L] glass Pyrex or large glass bowl and place the dough inside. Cover the bowl with a lid, plate, or plastic wrap and let it rest for 3 hours, or until doubled in volume.

-continued

To portion the matnakash, dust the counter lightly with flour and place the dough on top. Gently pat it into an oval. With a bench scraper or knife, cut the dough into two even pieces, about 1 lb [455 g] each. Using the sides of your palm, tuck the edges of the dough under to shape each portion into a round.

Dust a half-sheet pan with flour and place each round on top. Cover with a kitchen towel and let it rest for 1 hour, or until the dough is slightly puffy and springs back lightly when pressed.

To shape and bake, place a baking stone or baking steel in the bottom rack of the oven and remove the middle rack. Preheat the oven to 450°F [230°C]. Alternatively, use an overturned half-sheet pan in place of a baking stone (see page 41).

Dust the counter with flour and place the dough portions on top. Coat the same sheet pan that held the proofing dough with the wheat bran. In a bowl, mix together the ½ cup [70 g] all-purpose flour and the water.

Dip your hands into the water-flour mixture to coat thoroughly. For each portion of dough, you will make a ring on top with a tic-tac-toe pattern in the center of the ring. Start by cupping your hands and hold them perpendicular above the edges of the dough, as if you were gauging the size. Move your hands about 1 in [2.5 cm] in from the edges and press down firmly with the sides of your palms. This creates a ring inside the dough. Next, make the tic-tac-toe pattern. Wet your hands again and, using the sides of

one palm, make three lines within the circle. Wet your hand again and make three more lines in a grid pattern. Lift the dough onto the wheat bran–covered sheet pan and repeat with the second portion. Cover loosely with a kitchen towel for 25 to 30 minutes to allow the dough to rest.

Use some of the wheat bran to dust a pizza peel or an overturned sheet pan. Pick up one of the portions of dough with both hands, supporting the bottom, and gently stretch the dough into an oval so it's about 13 in [33 cm] long. Place the dough on top of the prepared pizza peel. If this step sounds tricky, put the dough on the dusted pizza peel and stretch it into an oval without picking it up. Open the oven and, with a quick jerk, transfer the dough onto the pizza stone.

Bake for 20 to 25 minutes, or until the bread is a deep golden brown. Repeat with the remaining portion. Let cool completely. Dust off excess wheat bran from the bottom if necessary.

Slice the matnakhash to serve at the table. Alternatively, the bread keeps in a zip-top plastic bag on the counter for 3 days or frozen for up to 1 month.

Tonir Hats

Թոնիրի հաց

tonir bread

In Artsakh, lavash comes second in preference to *tonir hats*, a round, yeasted bread about as thick as focaccia baked against the walls of an above-ground tonir oven. Perfect with butter and jam for breakfast, the simple, crusty bread sustained us on our road trip from Artsakh back to Armenia on May 2, 2018, the day Armenia erupted in protests against the parliament for failing to vote in Nikol Pashinyan as prime minister. That morning, we picked up a stack of bread in Stepanakert, watching as the women stretched rounds of dough over a small, round batat before striking it against the oven walls. Several hours later, as we stood in the sun at a roadblock near the high-altitude mining town of Vardenis, we were glad for the snacks.

To make tonir hats at home, we use the recipe for Matnakash (page 68), modifying the shaping and baking technique at the end. We like the puffiness of the bread, though if you'd like it to be flatter, pierce the stretched dough several times with a fork before sliding it into the oven.

-continued

Makes 2

OLD DOUGH

1 cup [140 g] all-purpose flour

½ cup [120 ml] lukewarm water
(see page 38)

¼ tsp instant yeast

1 recipe Matnakash dough
(page 68)

DOUGH

1 cup [240 ml] lukewarm water
(see page 38)

1 tsp instant yeast

3 cups plus 2 Tbsp [440 g]
all-purpose flour, plus more for
dusting

1 Tbsp kosher salt

Follow the instructions for making Matnakash (see page 70) until the shape-and-bake step.

To shape and bake, place a baking stone or baking steel in the bottom rack of the oven and remove the middle rack. Preheat the oven to 500°F [260°C]. Alternatively, use an overturned half-sheet pan in place of a baking stone (see page 41).

Dust the counter with flour and place the dough portions on top. For each portion, gently stretch and pat the dough into a 10 in [25 cm] round as if you were making pizza. Ensure there is enough flour underneath the dough to keep it from sticking to the counter, then cover loosely with a kitchen towel and let it rest until slightly puffy, about 25 minutes.

Pick up one of the portions and gently stretch it into a 12 in [30.5 cm] round. Dust a pizza peel with flour and place one round on top. If this step sounds tricky, put the dough on the dusted pizza peel and stretch it into a round without picking it up. Open the oven and, with a quick jerk, transfer the round onto the pizza stone. Turn the oven down to 450°F [230°C].

Bake for 15 to 20 minutes, or until the top turns deeply golden brown. Remove from the oven and set on a cooling rack. Repeat with the remaining round. While the bread is still warm but cool enough to handle, dust any excess flour off the bottom of the bread.

Slice tonir hats or serve whole and allow guests to tear off pieces. Alternatively, the bread keeps in a zip-top plastic bag on the counter for 3 days or frozen for up to 1 month.

Arishta

Ա ր ի ց ա ա

traditional dried flour noodles

On a dead-end street in the village of Argel, clotheslines filled with what looks like pasta hang in front of nearly every house. This is *arishta*, a simple noodle made from a dough that resembles salty lavash. Manoush Avedisyan, a longtime resident, invited us into her arishta workspace to demonstrate how she makes the noodles. The first step is making a firm dough, which she kneads by placing it between two plastic sheets and walking over it several times. She leaves the dough to relax before rolling it out into sheets with a rolling pin. She then switches to a rolling pin with grooves, which cuts the dough into noodles.

-continued

Makes about 1 lb [455 g] pasta (serves 4 to 6)

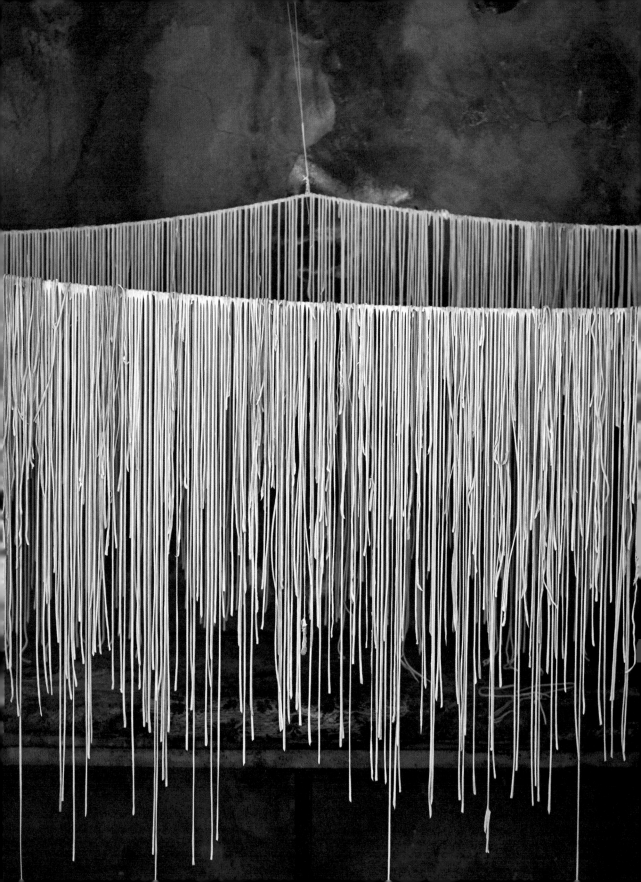

After they are cut, the noodles are hung out to dry overnight. In her house, stacks of dried arishta rest in bundles in a spare bedroom, and when orders come in, she toasts the strands to a golden color in an old Soviet toaster oven. We snacked on a couple of the strands, remarking how much they tasted like salty crackers. In Yerevan, arishta has become trendy, often served with wild mushrooms or cooked like a pilaf. But Manoush likes hers as simple as it gets: with butter on top and pickles on the side.

This is a project recipe, though it's a forgiving one. Make the dough and noodles the first day, then toast the noodles the second. At this point, you can store them, though they do tend to break into short sticks. See the Arishta with Mushrooms headnote (page 80) for how to cook the noodles.

3 cups [420 g] all-purpose flour, plus more for dusting

1 Tbsp kosher salt

¾ cup plus 2 Tbsp [210 ml] water, at room temperature

DAY ONE To make the dough, in a large bowl, mix together the flour and salt. Pour in the water and squish the flour and water together with your hands to form a shaggy dough. There will still be bits of flour at the bottom, and the dough will feel dry. Cover the bowl with a kitchen towel and let it rest for 20 minutes.

Uncover the bowl and check the consistency of the dough. It should feel softer and not quite as dry. At this point, either knead the dough in a stand mixer with a dough hook until it is smooth to the touch but not sticky, about 4 minutes, or knead it by hand until it reaches the same consistency, about 8 minutes. Let the dough rest for at least 1 hour or up to 2 hours.

To roll and cut the dough, clear off a large counter area and dust it with flour. Have a rolling pin and a few clean clothes hangers ready.

Uncover the dough, cut it into quarters, and pat each quarter into a rectangle. Working with one quarter at a time, roll the dough out until it's roughly 14 in [35.5 cm] long and 8 in [25 cm] wide. If the dough springs back and resists being rolled out, let it rest and start working on a different piece.

Once the piece has been rolled out, dust it generously with flour. Starting at a narrow end, roll up the dough into a cylinder. With a sharp knife,

cut the cylinder crosswise into strips ½ in [1 cm] wide. Unroll the strips quickly to keep them from sticking together. Shake off any excess flour and, one at a time, drape the noodles over the clothes hanger. The noodles will stretch a bit as they hang, but if some ends look too thick, trim them with scissors. Repeat with the remaining dough.

To dry the arishta, hang the noodles in a dry area overnight, putting a sheet pan underneath to catch any fallen strands.

DAY TWO To toast the arishta, preheat the oven to 350°F [180°C]. Break the noodles off the hangers (the noodles will be brittle, making it hard to remove them in one piece; it's okay if some pieces are smaller than others). Divide them between two half-sheet pans and bake until the noodles are golden and slightly toasted around the edges, about 12 minutes. Let cool completely on the pans.

The noodles can be stored for a month in a sealed container in the pantry, though they are fragile. To cook, boil the noodles in unsalted water, stirring often, for 4 minutes or until cooked through.

Arishta with Mushrooms

Անկով արիշտա

flour noodles with mushrooms

Although arishta, Armenia's answer to dried artisan noodles, has become common in trendy Yerevan restaurants, its roots lie in country cooking. It can be broken up into pieces and cooked with rice like pilaf or boiled like Italian pasta and served with mushrooms, like it is in this recipe. It's also common to see arishta topped with thin slices of *ghaurma*, a style of preserved beef in clarified butter. No matter how it's prepared, "there should be butter to make it tasty," says Manoush Avedisyan, the arishta maker who showed us her recipe for the dish.

Serves 4

What differentiates arishta from other noodles made of flour is the amount of salt; arishta itself contains enough that you don't need to salt the cooking water. To skip making arishta from scratch, try this workaround: Take good-quality store-bought tagliatelle or fettuccine and toast the noodles at 350°F [180°C] until light golden brown, 8 to 10 minutes. Then cook the noodles as directed on the package, with a few hearty pinches of salt in the cooking water.

2 lb [908 g] mushrooms, preferably oyster mushrooms or a mix

3 Tbsp unsalted butter, plus more as needed

3 garlic cloves

Kosher salt

Ground black pepper

2 Tbsp chopped dill

1 cup [240 g] plain, whole-milk yogurt

12 oz [340 g] Arishta (page 76)

Wash the mushrooms and dry them well. Slice lengthwise through the stem into quarters or halves, if they are small. If the mushrooms are quite large, trim off the stems and slice them separately.

In a wide saucepan or large heavy-bottomed skillet, melt the butter over medium heat. Smash 2 garlic cloves with the flat side of a knife, add it to the pan, and cook gently until the butter begins to brown and turn aromatic, about 1 minute. Increase the heat to medium-high and add the mushrooms. Sauté, stirring often, until the mushrooms have given off most of their liquid and started to brown, about 5 minutes. Oyster mushrooms in particular shrink down quite a bit. Season with a pinch of salt and pepper and sprinkle the dill on top. Remove from the heat.

Bring a large pot of water to a boil. Meanwhile, grate the remaining garlic clove and mix with the yogurt in a small bowl.

Drop the arishta into the boiling water and cook, stirring often to keep the strands from sticking, until cooked through, about 4 minutes. (If using store-bought noodles, follow the cooking instructions on the package.) Ladle out ½ cup [120 ml] of the cooking water, then drain the noodles in a colander.

Return the arishta to the pot. Pour in ¼ cup [60 ml] of the reserved water and stir in the mushrooms. Taste, seasoning with more salt and pepper if needed. If the pasta seems dry, add more of the reserved water and simmer a little longer to help the flavors come together. For a true Armenian touch, you can also add more butter.

Divide the pasta among 4 bowls and offer the garlic yogurt at the table so everyone can season their own bowl to their liking.

Tatar Boraki

Թաթար բորակի

egg noodles with yogurt

Christine Goroyan, our translator, grew up in Yerevan, but her family comes from the northwest city of Gyumri. For her, these diamond-shaped buttery egg noodles topped with yogurt taste like childhood. In Armenian dictionaries, *tatar* means "quick" or "rapid," and we watched Armine Yeghiazaryan make, cut, and boil the noodles in under one hour at Villa Kars, a historic Gyumri property turned hotel. Yet the name may have been adapted from *tatar börek*, a stuffed noodle dish with yogurt that traveled from central Asia to present-day Turkey centuries ago. Compared to making fussier forms of fresh noodles, *tatar boraki* is forgiving. The noodles can also be boiled ahead of time, cooled on an oiled sheet pan, and refrigerated until needed. Reheat cooked noodles in boiling water for about 1 minute.

While we like a little garlic in the yogurt sauce, Christine prefers to leave it out.

-continued

Serves 4 to 6

**3 cups [420 g] all-purpose flour,
plus more for dusting**

**1 tsp kosher salt, plus more for
seasoning**

2 large eggs

**½ cup [120 ml] lukewarm water
(see page 38)**

**1 cup [240 g] plain, whole-milk
yogurt**

1 garlic clove, grated

¼ cup [56 g] unsalted butter

Ground black pepper

To make the dough, place the flour in a large, wide bowl and sprinkle it with salt. Make a well in the center of the flour and add the eggs. With a fork, gently whisk the eggs to break them up. Then gradually start whisking the eggs into the flour until about a quarter of the flour is mixed in. Add the water and continue to mix in the flour to form a shaggy dough. Press the dough into the base of the bowl to get as much of the flour to stick to it as possible. The dough will be dry, and not all of the flour will be incorporated, but that's okay.

Turn out the dough and extra flour onto a clean counter. Knead the dough by repeatedly rolling it forward with the heel of your hand and folding it over itself until the dough feels smoother, with most of the flour mixed into it. Cover the dough with an overturned bowl and let it rest for 15 minutes.

To roll and cut the dough, dust the counter generously with flour, place the dough on top, and pat it into a rectangle. Using a rolling pin, roll the dough into a sheet about ⅛ in [4 mm] thick, dusting it with more flour to prevent it from sticking to the counter as you roll it. (This makes it easier to cut the pasta.)

With a pizza cutter or a knife, cut the dough into strips 1 in [2.5 cm] thick. For the straightest cuts, run the pizza cutter along a ruler. Then cut the strips at a diagonal to make diamonds between 1 and 2 in [2.5 and 5 cm] long. The pieces don't have to look identical.

Bring a large pot of salted water to a boil. Meanwhile, mix the yogurt and garlic together in a small bowl.

Gently drop the pasta all at once into the boiling water and start a timer for 7 minutes. Bring the pot back to a boil, stirring frequently to keep the water from boiling over and the pasta from sticking. After 3 or 4 minutes, the pasta will float to the top of the water, but it needs to cook for 3 or 4 minutes more before it's done.

Meanwhile, melt the butter in a small saucepan. Have a warmed serving bowl ready.

Place a colander in the sink and drain the pasta. Shake off the excess water and place the pasta in the serving bowl. Pour the butter on top and season with salt. Offer the garlic yogurt, salt, and pepper at the table so everyone can season their own bowl to their liking.

Artsakh

When we crossed the border between Armenia and the Republic of Artsakh after sunset in November of 2017, villages disappeared, giving way to a forested no-man's-land illuminated by the Milky Way. After traveling for miles without passing a village, streetlights and sidewalks unexpectedly appeared, as if they were lifted out of a California suburb. In a way, they might have been—the Armenian diaspora supports infrastructure here. In 2017, a second road connecting Artsakh to Armenia opened up, with half of the construction costs paid for by fundraising telethons in Los Angeles. These two roads are the only way in and out of the republic; an airport stands deserted because planes can't land under the threat of gunfire.

Framed by snow-capped mountains, Artsakh is a rugged mix of meadows, forests, streams, and mountains that turns rich shades of yellow and red in the fall. Artsakh is the ancient Armenian name for the area, which changed in the fourteenth century to Nagorno Karabakh, a combination, one theory goes, of a Russian term for "mountainous" and a Persian-Turkish word meaning "black garden." Roots of the conflict here go back to the early twentieth century, when the Soviet Union drew the borders between Armenia and Azerbaijan, lumping an Armenian region into economically stronger Azerbaijan in 1921. When the Soviet Union fell, a war over the territory broke out between the two former Soviet republics, culminating in 1994 with an Armenian victory on the ground. The war has since turned into a frozen conflict that flares up along the border now and again,

yet most of the world still recognizes this region as a part of Azerbaijan.

Despite the bucolic countryside, the memory of conflict is fresh—as recently as 2016, a four-day war broke out on the border. On the outskirts of Stepanakert, the capital city, trucks filled with soldiers rumble by "Tatik-Papik" (Grandma-Grandpa), the nickname for a sculpture of two heads formally called We Are Our Mountains. In vineyards, men wear fatigues while tending the vines.

Yet there's also a lot of pride in being from this place. Those who move to Yerevan still think of themselves as Karabakian—from Karabakh (or Artsakh)—and they're quick to explain their food to anyone who asks. A tomato tastes more like a tomato, they say, thanks to the clay soils. Even the grapes that grow here yield a rich red wine, aged in barrels made with local Caucasian oak.

Time will tell what will happen to this little republic that sits in limbo, but the area has started to draw tourists who come for the history and end up staying for the cafés around Stepanakert's sparkling clean downtown. After picking up visitor visas at the small Ministry of Culture office (a visa from Artsakh will prohibit you from visiting Azerbaijan, we were warned), we walked to the central bazaar where a row of women make Jingalov Hats (page 58), flatbreads shaped like deflated footballs cooked on griddles. Filled with local herbs, these breads are a true taste of place. "Which herbs do you use?" we started to ask. "How do you shape the bread?" And before long, we'd received a master class in Artsakh's most renowned contribution to flatbreads.

Creating Abundance

Sides and Simple Meals

omewhere near the town of Stepanavan on the road between Alaverdi and Gyumri, we passed a group of women of all ages in a meadow gathering greens into bags slung around their shoulders. We pulled to the side of the road and walked over to see what they were picking: stinging nettles and sindrick, a bitter green that looks a little like ramps. They said they might turn the nettles into soup, while the sindrick would be blanched and served with a bit of vinegar drizzled on top. With a little know-how and effort, these foragers were creating abundance out of what looked like a pile of weeds.

Whether it's gathering greens, cooking a pot of beans and using it in a handful of dishes, working ahead to make pickles, or even salting meat to cure it, efforts like these make it possible to create variety in meals, no matter the occasion.

This chapter provides a mix of simple and multistep recipes, but what they all share is the feeling of abundance they provide at the table. Salads include the most classic and ubiquitous tomato-and-cucumber-filled Summer Salad (page 92), as well as heartier options, all of which can be mixed and matched with meals from the Feasting chapter. We also share everyday soups, the kind that are best made in small batches and come together fairly quickly. (For heartier stews and broths, see Chanakh, page 204, and Khash, page 156.) Simple preparations can be a springboard for other vegetable-centric dishes—cook a pot of beans, say, and use it to make a bean side dish (page 114) and a snack of beans wrapped in lavash.

The chapter concludes with ways to stock your refrigerator to ensure that there are always a few options on hand when a meal needs something extra. Every home in Armenia has a stash of pickles stored in Soviet-era *banka* jars, where cucumbers, cauliflower, peppers, carrots, and cabbage jockey for shelf space. Soaked in a salt-water or vinegar brine, the mild, tangy pickles are served with nearly every meal, especially in the winter and spring, when fresh local produce is harder to come by.

For more advanced preserving challenges, try making Armenia's favorite cured meats, such as cumin- and fenugreek-seasoned Basturma (page 138) and the cured sausage Soujuk (page 142)—both of which are phenomenal with scrambled eggs.

Summer Salad

Ամառային աղցան

Tomatoes and cucumbers are easy to find year-round in Armenia, where they're often simply sliced up and eaten like pieces of fruit. But there's no question that the best time to eat tomatoes and cucumbers—and this salad—is in the summer. With juicy tomatoes and crisp cucumbers, the recipe hardly needs anything else. The key is using equal parts tomatoes and cucumbers, ensuring you add more than one fresh herb (cilantro and dill or cilantro and opal basil are common combinations), and mixing in a little onion and sliced green pepper for texture and flavor.

Western Armenians dress their version with more vinegar or lemon juice, but Eastern Armenians often go lighter on the acidity. In this recipe, we add a splash of apple cider vinegar to perk things up, but by all means add lemon juice in place of—or alongside—the vinegar if you prefer a brighter-tasting salad. For an extra treat, serve bread alongside to soak up the juices left in the salad bowl.

-continued

Serves 4 to 6

4 large tomatoes, cut into 1 in [2.5 cm] chunks

4 Persian cucumbers or 2 large English cucumbers, skin on, cut into 1 in [2.5 cm] chunks

¼ yellow onion, thinly sliced

1 Anaheim pepper or other mild green pepper, cored, seeded, and thinly sliced crosswise

¼ cup [10 g] chopped cilantro

2 Tbsp chopped dill

2 Tbsp apple cider vinegar

2 Tbsp sunflower oil or other neutral oil

1 tsp kosher salt, plus more for seasoning

Pinch of ground black pepper, plus more for seasoning

In a large bowl, mix together the tomatoes, cucumbers, onion, Anaheim pepper, cilantro, and dill. Drizzle the vinegar and oil over the salad and season with salt and pepper. Mix everything together thoroughly. Taste, adding more salt or pepper if needed.

Salat Vinaigrette

Վինեգրետ

beets, beans, and potato salad

A remnant from Soviet days, this Russian creation has a misleading name—there isn't any vinaigrette. Instead, it's a tangy, hearty salad filled with cooked potatoes, beets, carrots, beans, and dill pickles that feels quite at home in an Armenian meal. It's also a great make-ahead salad, keeping for a few days in the refrigerator.

After spending an afternoon cooking and dicing the vegetables for this salad, Ara came up with an easier method: Dice the vegetables (with the exception of the beets) before they're cooked to save on cooking time and make them easier to dice. If you have Pickled Beets (page 136), save a step and use them in this salad. Alternatively, consider cooking more beets than what's called for in this recipe and use them elsewhere, such as in the Beet Greens Soup (page 105). Either canned or dried beans cooked from scratch work for this recipe. For guidance on cooking beans, see Cooking Dried Beans, page 32. Some dill pickles lack acidity. If you need to perk up the salad's tanginess, pour some of the pickle juice into the salad.

-continued

Serves 6

2 medium red beets, greens removed

2 carrots, peeled and diced into ½ in [12 mm] cubes

2 Yukon gold potatoes, peeled and diced into ½ in [12 mm] cubes

2 Tbsp sunflower oil or other neutral oil

¼ yellow onion, diced

One 15.5 oz [440 g] can cranberry beans or pinto beans, drained, or 1½ cup [360 ml] cooked homemade beans

2 dill pickles, diced into ½ in [12 mm] pieces

¼ cup [10 g] chopped cilantro

¼ cup [10 g] chopped dill

½ tsp kosher salt, plus more for seasoning

¼ tsp ground black pepper, plus more for seasoning

Wash the beets thoroughly to remove any mud or grit. In a small saucepan, cover the beets with water and bring to a boil. Lower to a gentle simmer, cover, and cook until the beets are tender when pierced with the tip of a knife, about 25 minutes. Drain. When the beets are cool enough to handle, use your fingers or a paring knife to slip off their skins. Discard the skins and dice the beets into ½ in [12 mm] cubes.

Place the carrots and potatoes in a soup pot. Cover with water and add a few pinches of salt. Bring the water to a boil, lower to a simmer, and cook until the potato pieces are tender when pierced with the tip of a knife, about 10 minutes. Drain and cool to room temperature.

Heat the oil in a sauté pan over medium heat. Add the onion and cook, stirring occasionally, until translucent, about 4 minutes.

Transfer the onion to a large mixing bowl. Mix in the beets, carrots, potatoes, beans, dill pickles, and herbs. Season with the salt and pepper, then taste, adding more salt or pepper, if desired. Serve at room temperature. Alternatively, the salad keeps, refrigerated, for up to 4 days.

Green Salad with Radishes

Բողկով կանաչ աղցան

Armenia's most common kind of lettuce looks like a smaller, more delicate head of romaine, and romaine or Little Gem lettuces (or a mix of the two) make a nice approximation of it. This simple salad is the perfect foil for the main courses in the Feasting chapter, especially Lavash-Wrapped Trout (page 183). Look for radishes with pretty greens—if they look bright and fresh, wash them well and mix them in with the lettuce. (Skip them if the leaves look tired or old.)

Serves 4

1 green onion, thinly sliced

1 Tbsp apple cider vinegar

1 Tbsp freshly squeezed lemon juice

1 tsp pomegranate molasses or a pinch of sugar

¼ tsp kosher salt, plus more for seasoning

¼ tsp sweet paprika

1 bunch radishes and their greens (about 6 radishes)

1 head romaine lettuce or a mix of romaine and Little Gem lettuces, coarsely chopped (about 8 cups [160 g])

2 Tbsp chopped mint

2 Tbsp sunflower oil or other neutral oil

Place the green onion in a small bowl and pour the vinegar and lemon juice on top. Season with the pomegranate molasses, salt, and paprika, and let sit for at least 5 minutes to draw out the flavors.

Cut the radishes into wedges and coarsely chop the radish greens, if using.

Place the radishes and radish greens, lettuce, and mint in a salad bowl. Season with a pinch of salt.

In the bowl with the green onion, whisk in the oil with a fork. Pour the vinaigrette over the lettuce. Using clean hands or a pair of tongs, mix the greens well so that they are evenly coated in the vinaigrette. Taste a piece of lettuce and season with more salt or vinegar, if desired.

"Aveluk Salad"

Կերծ ավելուկով աղցան

One of the most notable salads in Armenia is built around *aveluk*, a dried sour herb that is rehydrated and mixed with walnuts and occasionally pomegranate seeds. You're usually given the option of mixing in yogurt, too—which, in our opinion, makes the salad come to life. Because finding aveluk outside of Armenia is not an easy task, this recipe is our "aveluk salad." Earthy beet greens and green Swiss chard give a similar texture to rehydrated aveluk leaves, while the vinegar adds a sour accent. If some of the beet greens look scrawny, you can bulk them up with other hearty greens, such as mustard greens. Mix half of the garlic yogurt into the greens and serve the rest on the side to add as desired.

Serves 4

1 bunch red beets, with greens attached

1 bunch green Swiss chard or mustard greens

⅛ yellow onion, thinly sliced

2 Tbsp apple cider vinegar

2 Tbsp sunflower oil or other neutral oil

1 tsp pomegranate molasses

½ tsp kosher salt

¼ tsp ground black pepper

½ cup [120 g] plain, whole-milk yogurt

1 small garlic clove, grated

½ cup [55 g] walnut halves, lightly toasted

¼ cup [30 g] pomegranate seeds

Trim away the beets from the greens and save for another use. Wash the greens (including the stems) thoroughly to remove any mud or grit, and do the same with the Swiss chard. For all of the greens, cut the stems into 1 in [2.5 cm] pieces and slice the greens into thick ribbons. You should have about 8 cups [440 g] of greens.

Bring a pot of water to a boil. Add the stems to the water and cook for 1 minute. Stir in the greens and cook until wilted, another 30 seconds. Drain well in a colander, pressing on the greens with a spoon to remove extra water. Let cool to room temperature.

Meanwhile, in a small bowl, soak the onion slices in the vinegar for at least 5 minutes or longer. Stir in the oil, pomegranate molasses, salt,

and pepper to make a dressing. In a separate small bowl, mix together the yogurt and garlic.

Place the greens and stems in a serving bowl. Mix in the onion-vinegar dressing, walnuts, and half of the garlic yogurt. Sprinkle the pomegranate seeds on top and serve the remaining yogurt on the side. Leftover salad keeps, refrigerated, for up to 3 days.

Spas

Ս պ ա ս

yogurt soup

Given the probiotic benefits of yogurt, it makes sense to call this yogurt soup *spas*—at least from an American point of view. The reality is that yogurt soups have been an important part of Eastern and Western Armenian traditions going back centuries, though Western Armenians call their version *tanabour*. Armenian cookbooks attribute the tradition of yogurt soups to Van and Erzurum, cities that were the center of Armenian culture in the fifteenth and sixteenth centuries. Today it's common to add rice to spas, but the more traditional versions contain wheat berries, which take longer to cook. We've compromised with this soup by using pearled farro, which cooks in a shorter amount of time but imparts a chewy texture similar to wheat berries. Barley works as well, giving a similar texture to the soup.

-continued

Serves 4

The key to making spas is to avoid scrambling the eggs, which are added to give the soup a silky texture. There are a lot of myths about how to avoid doing so (one is that you must constantly stir the soup with a specific wooden spoon), but the reality is less complicated: Make sure you stir the pot while slowly pouring in the mixture. To make it easier to pour the mixture into the pot, put it into a pitcher or large liquid measuring cup. If you don't have a large enough one, refill it as you work. If you have leftovers, try it cold, another traditional way to eat spas.

¾ cup [150 g] pearled farro or barley

6 cups [1.4 L] water

2 tsp kosher salt

4 cups [960 g] plain, whole-milk yogurt

½ cup [120 g] sour cream

2 large eggs

2 Tbsp unsalted butter

½ yellow onion, finely diced

½ cup [20 g] chopped cilantro

Ground black pepper

Place the farro and 3 cups [720 ml] of the water in a soup pot with 1 tsp of the salt and bring to a boil. Lower to a simmer and cook, uncovered, until the farro is cooked through but still chewy in the center, about 20 minutes. Turn off the heat and let the grains cool in the water for 5 minutes.

Meanwhile, in a large bowl, whisk together the yogurt, sour cream, eggs, remaining 1 tsp salt, and remaining 3 cups [720 ml]

water until smooth. Transfer to a pitcher or liquid measuring cup.

Stirring constantly, pour the yogurt mixture into the pot with the farro in a thin, continuous stream. Turn the heat to medium-high until the yogurt begins to foam up and boil on the edges. Stir constantly to ensure the soup stays creamy and the eggs cook evenly. Lower the heat to a gentle simmer and cook for 5 to 10 minutes to thicken the soup further. Turn off the heat but leave the pot on the stove.

In a sauté pan over medium-high heat, melt the butter. Add the onion and sauté until softened and just beginning to brown, 4 to 5 minutes. Pour the onion and any remaining butter into the soup and stir in the cilantro. The surface of the soup may have beads of oil; don't worry, it's perfectly fine. Season with pepper.

To serve, gently rewarm the soup if needed and ladle it into warmed bowls. Serve leftovers chilled or rewarmed the next day.

Beet Greens Soup

Բազուկով ապուր

In the mountain town of Dilijan, chef Alex Ghazaryan demonstrated a decidedly South Caucasus take on beet soup at Tufenkian Old Dilijan Complex, a hotel. His version takes the idea of borscht but places more emphasis on the beet greens, not the beets. Alex also adds pomegranate molasses and fresh mint, which brighten the otherwise earthy, sweet flavors of the beets.

Make this soup in two parts, cooking the split peas and rice in the soup pot and the beets in a separate pot. The beets can be cooked a few days before making the soup—in fact, if you have cooked beets left over from a different recipe, use them in this soup. If the beet greens are scraggly, you can use a bunch of green Swiss chard instead. Leftover meat from Khashlama (page 208) can be added to beef up the flavor, though the soup is equally satisfying without it.

-continued

Serves 4

2 Tbsp sunflower oil or other neutral oil

1 yellow onion, finely diced

½ cup [100 g] yellow split peas

2 tsp kosher salt, plus more for seasoning

8 cups [2 L] water

1 bunch red beets, with greens attached (about 3 beets total)

3 or 4 sorrel leaves (optional), sliced

¼ cup [50 g] long-grain rice

1 bay leaf

1 cup [150 g] sliced cooked beef (optional)

1 Tbsp pomegranate molasses

1 Tbsp chopped mint, for serving

Heat the oil in a soup pot over medium-high heat. Stir in the onion and sweat until softened but before it begins to brown, about 4 minutes. Add the split peas, 1 tsp of the salt, and the water and bring to a boil. Lower the heat to a simmer and cook gently until the split peas are softened but not fully cooked in the center, about 35 minutes. Turn off the heat but keep the pot on the stove.

Meanwhile, trim away the beets from the stems, then cut the stems from the greens. Wash the beets, the stems, and the greens thoroughly to remove any mud or grit. In a separate soup pot or saucepan with a lid, cover the beets with water and bring to a boil. Lower to a gentle simmer, cover, and cook until the beets are tender when pierced with the tip of a knife, about 25 minutes. Drain.

When the beets are cool enough to handle, use your fingers or a paring knife to slip off their skins. Discard the skins and dice the beets into pieces that will fit on a soup spoon.

Cut the stems of the greens into 1 in [2.5 cm] pieces and slice the greens into thick ribbons. You should have about 6 cups [330 g] of greens.

Bring the pot with the split peas back to a simmer. Stir in the sorrel, if using, the rice, stems, greens, diced beets, bay leaf, and remaining 1 tsp salt. Cook until the rice and split peas are cooked all the way through, about 20 minutes. Stir in the beef, if using, and pomegranate molasses. Bring to a boil, lower to a simmer, and cook until the meat is hot all the way through. Taste, seasoning with more salt, if desired.

Ladle into 4 soup bowls and sprinkle mint on top to serve. Leftover soup keeps, refrigerated, for up to 1 week. Bring to a simmer with a splash of water before serving. (The rice and split peas absorb broth over time.)

Konchol

Կոնչոլ

day-old bread soup

Born out of a need to use up old bread, this soup falls into the same category as Italian ribollita or Portuguese bread soup. For that reason, it is a something-from-nothing kind of soup, the sort of dish that can be made quickly with a few other ingredients that you likely already have on hand: an onion, a little butter, and a couple of eggs. The most classic broth for *konchol* is simply water, but the soup is excellent with chicken broth, too. It's traditional to mix the bread into the pot before serving, but putting the bread in each serving bowl and pouring the soup over the top gives a nice contrast in textures.

Leftover Matnakash (page 68) or Tonir Hats (page 73) are both perfect for this recipe, though country-style French bread works well, too. The soup only serves two, with the idea that it's best eaten soon after making. If serving more people, simply double the recipe.

-continued

Serves 2

2 cups [70 g] cubed day-old bread

2 Tbsp unsalted butter

1 yellow onion, thinly sliced

1¼ tsp kosher salt

¼ tsp ground black pepper

5 cups [1.2 L] chicken broth or water

2 large eggs

2 Tbsp chopped cilantro

2 Tbsp chopped dill

2 Tbsp chopped flat-leaf parsley

In a toaster oven or an oven preheated to 350°F [180°C], toast the bread until crunchy all the way through and slightly brown on top, about 8 minutes. Set aside.

Heat the butter in a soup pot over medium heat. Stir in the onion, 1 tsp of the salt, and the pepper, decrease the heat to low, and sweat the onion, stirring often, until it is soft and beginning to brown on the edges, 8 to 10 minutes. Pour in the broth and bring to a boil. Lower to a simmer and cook for 5 minutes to concentrate the flavors of the broth.

In a small bowl, beat the eggs with a fork and season with the remaining ¼ tsp salt. While stirring the broth, pour in the eggs and cook until the eggs float to the top, about 1 minute. Stir in the herbs.

Divide the bread between 2 serving bowls. Ladle the soup on top and serve immediately. This soup is best the day it is made.

Meatball Soup

Կոլոլակով ապուր

If your restaurant is always busy, does it need a name? Stepan Garaghanyan doesn't think so. He's run his always-busy Yerevan lunch spot on Marx Street next door to the tax authority for nearly a decade without one. Whenever we've gone for lunch, a clientele of tough-looking guys hunched over bowls of soup sat in contrast to the delicate decor: a china cabinet in the back and oil paintings lining the walls. John thinks these guys come because Garaghanyan's no-name restaurant specializes in food that tastes like Mom made it, and that theory might not be too far off—apart from Stepan, the restaurant has an all-female cast. Manager Angela Sahakyan takes orders and delivers plates to tables while Anahit Manukyan, a former post office manager, runs the kitchen. Manukyan always makes soup, including Spas (page 102) and this recipe.

One yellow onion is used in two places here—the meatball mix and the broth. Homemade chicken broth makes a great base for this soup, though the restaurant simply adds bouillon to water. If using bouillon instead of chicken broth, cut the amount of salt added to the soup in half; you can always add more salt later if you'd like.

-continued

Serves 4

MEATBALLS

1 lb [455 g] lean ground beef

¼ cup [50 g] long-grain white rice

¼ yellow onion, finely chopped

1 large egg

2 Tbsp chopped dill

2 Tbsp chopped cilantro or parsley

2 garlic cloves, minced

1 tsp kosher salt

¼ tsp ground black pepper

SOUP

1 Tbsp sunflower oil or other neutral oil

¾ yellow onion, finely chopped

2 garlic cloves, minced

1 bay leaf

2 tsp kosher salt

½ tsp sweet paprika

8 cups [2 L] chicken broth or water

1 Yukon gold potato, peeled and cubed

1 carrot, peeled and sliced into coins

1 red bell or Anaheim pepper, cored, seeded, and thinly sliced

¼ cup [10 g] chopped dill

¼ cup [10 g] chopped cilantro or flat-leaf parsley

Opal basil leaves, torn (optional)

Ground black pepper

To make the meatballs, oil a large plate. In a large bowl, using your hands, thoroughly mix the meat, rice, onion, egg, dill, cilantro, garlic, salt, and pepper. The mixture will feel sticky at first. Roll the mixture into 12 balls and transfer to the prepared plate. (To make it easier to shape the meatballs, wet your hands with water as you work.)

To make the soup, in a soup pot, heat the oil over medium heat. Add the onion, garlic, and bay leaf. Sweat, stirring occasionally, until the onion softens, about 4 minutes. Stir in the salt and paprika and cook for 30 more seconds. Pour in the broth and bring to a boil. Lower to a simmer and cook for 5 minutes.

Add the meatballs to the water one by one to prevent them from sticking together. Bring the soup to a boil, then decrease the heat to medium-low and gently simmer, stirring occasionally, for 15 minutes.

Add the potato and cook for another 10 minutes, or until the meat is cooked through and the rice inside the meatball is nearly all the way cooked (you can cut one of the meatballs in half to check). Add the carrot and bell pepper, cover, and let sit for 10 minutes.

To serve, bring to a simmer. Ladle into bowls, serving 3 meatballs per person. Sprinkle each serving with dill, cilantro, and basil, if using, and finish with a pinch of black pepper. Extra soup keeps, refrigerated, for up to 5 days.

Goris Beans

Գորիսի լոբի

Beans from the city of Goris are legendary for their deep flavor and creamy texture. Like cranberry beans and pinto beans, they're speckled when dry but turn one uniform color when cooked. Yet the range of colors and sizes varies quite a bit. Some are light reddish-pink, similar in size to pinto beans, while others are deeply purple and large enough to creep into lima-bean territory. We were once held captive at lunch while women from Goris explained the nuances between the beans grown in specific villages around the city. Much of the detail was lost in translation (everyone spoke at once, and Goris residents are famous for their strong accents). What wasn't lost was the pride they had for local beans, and deservedly so; the beans taste so rich on their own that the best preparations are simple ones, like this recipe.

-continued

Serves 4 to 6

If using dried beans, start with 1½ cups [240 g]; see Cooking Dried Beans (page 32). Reserve some of the bean cooking water to add to the pot. While this recipe is written to mash the beans to the consistency of refried beans, the beans can also be left whole and served at room temperature with a little lemon juice. Leftover beans can be turned into the filling for Bean Lavash Triangles (page 117).

2 Tbsp sunflower oil or other neutral oil

1 yellow onion, thinly sliced

Two 15.5 oz [440 g] cans cranberry or pinto beans, drained, or 3 cups [720 g] cooked homemade beans

2 tsp kosher salt (or 1 tsp if the canned beans are salty)

1 cup [240 ml] water or bean cooking water

¼ tsp ground black pepper

¼ tsp crushed dried red pepper (optional)

¾ cup [30 g] chopped cilantro

¼ cup [10 g] chopped dill

Lavash (page 48) and sheep's milk feta (optional), for serving

Heat the oil in a pot over medium heat. Add the onion and cook, stirring often, until translucent and starting to brown on the edges, about 5 minutes.

Add the beans and 1 tsp of the salt and begin to smash them with a potato masher or a wooden spoon. Once the beans have been broken up into pieces, pour in the water or bean cooking water and bring to a simmer. Cook the beans, stirring constantly, until they thicken up to the

consistency of chunky refried beans. Season with the remaining 1 tsp of salt, if desired, and the pepper and mix in the herbs. Serve hot alongside lavash and cheese, if using. Leftover beans keep, refrigerated, for up to 1 week.

Bean Lavash Triangles

Լավաշի երանկյունիներ լոբով

The afternoon we spent cooking with Anahit Badalyan at her home in Goris, we thought she'd eventually run out of things to make with the big batch of beans she had cooked. We had challenged her the day before to show us all the ways you can use the city's famous legumes, and two slam dunks in (a bean side dish and a bean salad), we figured we had maxed out. But then she started mashing beans and wrapping them in lavash. The resulting triangles (we called them "bean samosas") may have been *the* favorite bean recipe of the day.

-continued

Serves 6 to 8

If using dried beans, start with 1½ cups [240 g]; see Cooking Dried Beans (page 32). Buy the thinnest, most pliable lavash you can find. If using homemade Lavash (page 48), keep it covered to prevent it from drying out. If it starts to crack, spritz it with water, cover with a towel, and let it sit for a few minutes to soften up.

¼ cup plus 2 Tbsp [90 ml] sunflower oil or other neutral oil, plus more as needed

½ yellow onion, finely diced

Two 15.5 oz [440 g] cans cranberry or pinto beans, drained, or 3 cups [720 g] cooked homemade beans

1 tsp kosher salt

½ tsp ground black pepper

2 Tbsp chopped cilantro

1 Tbsp chopped dill

4 large sheets Lavash (page 48)

To make the filling, in a medium saucepan over medium-high heat, warm 2 Tbsp [30 ml] of the oil. Stir in the onion, lower the heat to medium, and cook, stirring occasionally, until translucent, about 4 minutes. Stir in the beans, salt, and pepper and cook until the beans absorb some of the seasoning and are hot all the way through, about 2 minutes. Turn off the heat.

Using a potato masher or an immersion blender, mash the beans in the pot to make a paste. Mash in the cilantro and dill and let cool to room temperature.

Cut the lavash into 12 strips 3 in [7.5 cm] thick and about 12 in [30.5 cm] long. Keep cut lavash covered or in a plastic bag so the strips don't dry out.

To shape each triangle, position a strip of lavash in front of you vertically. Place about 2 Tbsp of bean paste at the bottom end of the strip. Pull the bottom left corner of the strip to the right side, about 3 in [7.5 cm] up from the bottom, to create a triangle that encases the beans. Next, take the bottom right corner of the triangle and fold it away from you to the left edge of the lavash to enclose the filling, "rolling" the triangle up the lavash and adding a layer to the triangle. Continue to fold the triangle all the way up the strip until all of the lavash is used up. If any extra lavash hangs off the edge, trim it with scissors. Once finished, place the triangle seam-side down and repeat with the remaining strips and filling.

Line a plate with paper towels. Heat 2 Tbsp of oil in a large sauté pan over medium-high heat. Place half of the triangles seam-side down in the oil and fry until golden brown on one side, about 1 minute, adjusting the heat as needed to prevent the lavash from burning. Flip the triangles over to brown the other side, 30 seconds to 1 minute more. Transfer to the paper towel–lined plate and repeat with the remaining oil and triangles. If the pan seems too dry after flipping over the triangles, add more oil. Let cool slightly before serving. Leftovers keep, refrigerated, for up to 3 days and can be reheated in a toaster oven for 3 to 5 minutes until hot in the center.

Eggs Three Ways

While packing up the apartment we rented in Alaverdi, a northern copper mining town near the Georgian border, our host started preparing us a plate of greens and eggs so we didn't hit the road on empty stomachs. Eggs with "fill-in-the-blank" is so common in Armenia that it's nearly always the answer when a quick and healthy meal is called for. It's also a great way to use up whatever is in the kitchen, and any time we asked what to do with an unfamiliar green, the answer was always "cook it with eggs." Greens aren't the only ingredient added to these informal egg scrambles. Tomatoes are common, and so are cured meats, such as Basturma (page 138) or Soujuk (page 142), both of which you can find at Middle Eastern markets.

In Alaverdi, our dish was a lot of greens and only a little egg, which was likely a way to stretch protein to feed more people but could also be seen as a way to eat more vegetables. Either way, the idea is to make use of what you have on hand. Use more greens or tomatoes and fewer eggs if you wish. A side of Lavash (page 48), Matnakash (page 68), or Tonir Hats (page 73) makes the meal complete.

-continued

Serves 2 or 3

Greens with Eggs

Կանաչիով ձվածեղ

1 Tbsp sunflower oil or other neutral oil

2 green onions, thinly sliced, or
¼ yellow onion, finely diced

4 cups [220 g] chopped greens
(such as spinach, dandelion greens,
or chard), coarse stems removed or
finely sliced

4 large eggs, beaten with a fork

¼ tsp kosher salt

Pinch of ground black pepper

1 Tbsp chopped dill, for serving

Heat the oil in a large nonstick skillet over medium heat. Add the green onions and cook until slightly softened, about 30 seconds. Add the greens and cook, stirring, until wilted.

Pour in the eggs and season with the salt and pepper. Gently stir the eggs until they begin to set. Turn off the heat, stir the eggs again, and let them finish cooking to your liking. Sprinkle with the dill before serving.

Tomatoes with Eggs

Լոլիկով ձվածեղ

1 Tbsp sunflower oil or other neutral oil

3 large tomatoes, diced

4 large eggs, beaten with a fork

¼ tsp kosher salt

Pinch of ground black pepper

2 Tbsp chopped cilantro or flat-leaf
parsley (or both), for serving

Heat the oil in a large nonstick skillet over medium heat. Add the tomatoes, and cook, breaking up the tomato pieces with a spoon, until the tomato juices have thickened, 1 to 2 minutes.

Pour in the eggs and season with salt and pepper. Gently stir the eggs until they begin to set. Turn off the heat, stir the eggs again, and let them finish cooking to your liking. Sprinkle with the cilantro before serving.

Basturma with Eggs

Բաստուրմայով ձվածեղ

1 Tbsp sunflower oil or other neutral oil

6 thin slices Basturma (page 138)

5 large eggs, beaten with a fork

Kosher salt

Ground black pepper

1 green onion, thinly sliced

Heat the oil in a large nonstick skillet over medium heat. Lay the basturma in the pan in an even layer, trying not to overlap the pieces too much, and cook until the meat begins to sizzle.

Flip the basturma pieces over. Pour in the eggs, season with a modest pinch of salt and pepper (the basturma is salty), and gently stir until the eggs begin to set. Turn off the heat, stir the eggs again, and let them finish cooking to your liking. Sprinkle green onion on top before serving.

Marinated Trout

Մարինացված իշխան

Falling somewhere between gravlax and escabeche, this cured trout preparation, in which fish is "cooked" in salt and vinegar, makes for an impressive addition to a table filled with the usual—lavash, pickles, cucumbers and tomatoes, and an herb and cheese plate. The salty, tangy trout is a perfect appetizer for a party, and it can be made up to 4 days ahead of time. Rip off a small piece of lavash, place a couple of pieces of trout on top, roll it up, and you have the Armenian answer to a hand roll.

-continued

Serves 6 as an appetizer

A note of caution on trout: We were introduced to this idea at Cherkezi Dzor, a restaurant and fish hatchery in Gyumri, where the fish was caught and cured in one place, allowing the quality of the fish to be controlled. To be on the safe side, choose sustainably farmed trout for this recipe and save any wild specimens you catch for the grill or stove—wild freshwater fish can carry parasites if eaten raw.

1½ lb [680 g] butterflied (nearly boneless) trout (3 to 4 fish)

¼ cup [40 g] kosher salt

2 Tbsp apple cider vinegar

2 Tbsp water

1 cup [150 g] thinly sliced yellow onion

¾ cup [100 g] thinly sliced carrots

10 allspice berries

1 bay leaf

2 Tbsp chopped dill

1½ tsp granulated sugar

¼ tsp ground black pepper

To skin each trout, open the belly up and cut the spine out to make two separate fillets. With the fish skin-side down, hold the tail end of the fish with one hand while holding the knife in the other. Aim the blade of the knife down toward the skin at a slight angle facing away from the tail to make the first incision and then run the blade parallel along the skin to separate the skin from the flesh. Discard the skin and cut the trout into 1 in [2.5 cm] pieces.

In a medium glass mixing bowl, mix together the trout and salt until the salt coats the trout pieces evenly. Mix in the remaining ingredients, then cover the bowl with plastic wrap and refrigerate for 24 hours.

After 24 hours, the trout is ready to eat. Alternatively, it will keep, refrigerated, for up to 5 days.

Chikufta

Ջի ֆյուֆթա

beef tartare with bulgur

"Hands down, my favorite dish growing up was my mom's *chikufta*," Ara told us soon after we started working together. "Whenever I saw her preparing it, I would bounce around the kitchen until it was served," he said. This is one of the reasons we included this Western Armenian raw beef and bulgur dish in our book. The other reason is that chikufta (written countless other ways, such as *chikefte* and *chikofte*) is becoming more common in Yerevan. At Zeituna, a Western Armenian restaurant run by the Syrian-Armenian Rastkelenian family, it's one of the most popular dishes on the menu.

-continued

Serves 6 to 8

The key to successful chikufta is to use the right kind of meat, which needs to be very fresh, extremely lean, and ground almost as fine as a paste. Look for ground meat prepared for chikufta at Middle Eastern butchers, where it comes ready to be mixed and seasoned. Ara's mom, Maggie Zada, presents the dish one of two ways: either spread out on a plate and embossed with a checkered design (which is how our recipe is written), or what Ara calls "squishy" because it requires squeezing the meat into little footballs with finger indentations (pictured on page 127). Chikufta should be eaten the day it's made, though any extra can be fried up into patties and served as cooked *kufta* the next day.

¾ cup [120 g] medium-grain bulgur

2 cups [480 ml] water

1 yellow onion, finely diced

2 Tbsp red pepper paste

2 tsp kosher salt

1 tsp ground coriander

1 tsp ground cumin

¼ tsp ground allspice

2 lb [908 g] chikufta meat (see headnote)

3 green onions, thinly sliced

¼ cup [10 g] finely chopped flat-leaf parsley

Sunflower oil or olive oil, for drizzling

Lavash (page 48), for serving

In a bowl, soak the bulgur in the water for 15 minutes, or until the bulgur has plumped up and absorbed most of the water.

Have a small bowl of cold water and a large mixing bowl ready. While the bulgur soaks, mix the onion, pepper paste, salt, and spices together in the large bowl. Chill a large dinner plate.

With clean hands, scoop the bulgur out of the water and squeeze out as much water as possible. Place the bulgur in the bowl on top of the spices and put the meat on top. Knead by pressing the ingredients into the base of the bowl, folding the mixture over, and repeating until the chikufta feels sticky, about 5 minutes. As you work, dip your hands in the cold water periodically to keep the meat from sticking to your hands and to keep the meat cold.

Lightly oil the chilled plate (this keeps the chikufta from sticking to it). Pat the chikufta out until it's about 1 in [2.5 cm] thick. Using wet hands, smooth out the surface. Drag the flat side of a fork's tines (not the sharp points), across the top to make a crisscross pattern.

Mix the green onions and parsley together and sprinkle along the edges to make a green border. Cover with plastic wrap and refrigerate for at least 30 minutes or up to 4 hours so the bulgur can absorb the seasonings.

Right before serving, remove the plastic wrap and drizzle the top with a little oil to make the surface shine. Spoon onto plates and eat with torn pieces of lavash.

Eech

ԻՉ

tomato and bulgur salad

The meat-free version of Chikufta (page 126), *eech* is on every Western
Armenain wedding table and party spread. And with good reason: If you're
feeding a vegetarian crowd—or you want more vegetarian options on the
table—this make-ahead side dish is perfect for entertaining. With tomatoes
taking the place of ground meat, it's also a visually striking dish that delivers whole-grain goodness thanks to bulgur, which also gives this vegetable
side dish texture. It can hold up well at room temperature in case the party
lasts all day.

-continued

Serves 6

6 Roma tomatoes

1 Tbsp sunflower oil or olive oil, plus more for garnish

1 yellow onion, finely chopped

½ cup [120 ml] water

¼ cup [60 g] tomato paste

1 Tbsp red pepper paste (optional)

2½ tsp kosher salt, plus more for seasoning

½ tsp ground cumin

1½ cups [240 g] medium-grain bulgur

3 green onions, thinly sliced

1 cup [40 g] finely chopped flat-leaf parsley

¼ cup [60 ml] lemon juice

Bring a pot of water to a boil. Have a slotted spoon and a bowl of ice water handy.

Using a sharp knife, cut a small *X* into the bottom of each tomato and then cut out the stem end, taking care not to remove too much of the tomato. Add the tomatoes to the water and cook briefly until the skin starts to lift from the *X*, about 30 seconds. Lift the tomatoes out of the pot and plunge them into the ice water.

Once cool enough to handle, peel and discard the skins from the tomatoes. The skins should slide right off. If some pieces are stubborn, either cut them off or put the tomatoes back into the boiling water for a few more seconds and chill them in the ice water again. Finely dice the tomatoes, keeping their seeds and juices.

Heat the oil in a large sauté pan over medium heat. Add the onion and cook, stirring occasionally, until translucent, about 4 minutes. Add the water and the tomatoes with their juices and bring to a simmer. Lower the heat, cover the pan, and simmer gently until the tomatoes have softened, 5 minutes.

Uncover the pan and stir in the tomato paste, pepper paste, if using, salt, and cumin.

Pour the contents of the pan into a large mixing bowl. Mix in the bulgur and let the mixture sit for 30 minutes, or until the bulgur has plumped up and absorbed the water and tomato juices.

Leave a little green onion and parsley behind for garnishing the top, and mix the rest into the bulgur, along with half of the lemon juice. Using clean hands, knead and press the mixture together in the bowl until the bulgur absorbs more of the seasonings, about 3 minutes. Taste, adding more lemon juice or salt, if desired.

Spread the eech onto a large rimmed plate and garnish with the remaining green onion and parsley. Drizzle the top with oil to make the surface shine, if desired. Leftovers keep, refrigerated, for up to 1 week. Serve leftovers chilled or at room temperature.

Small-Batch Pickles

Fermenting vegetables isn't as technical as many fear. If you're new to it, the small-batch recipes for lacto-fermented (salt-brined) pickles in this book are just enough to give you a feel for the process. If you catch the fermenting bug, you can double or triple the recipe, fermenting vegetables in larger batches.

For the salt-brined pickles in this book, use a widemouthed mason jar with a 4 cup [960 ml] capacity. To ensure that the vegetables stay submerged in the brine as they ferment (this keeps undesirable bacteria and mold away), you need to weigh them down. In Armenia, some use a stone, but lids work as well, as do zip-top bags filled with extra salt brine. We find that stacking a few smaller lids inside the mason jar does the job.

You also need a lid that allows gas to escape during fermentation. The easiest solution is an inexpensive silicone airlock, which looks like a regular lid save for a small opening at the top that allows gas to release. If you don't have an airlock, you can use a regular lid as long as you remember to open the jar once a day to "burp" it.

No less valuable on the table than their salt-brined cousins, vinegar-brined pickles are another way to ensure you always have a side of vegetables to offer friends and family while they're eating lavash.

-continued

If you see a little mold on the surface, scrape it off. Otherwise, keep the jar covered. You'll know the fermentation is working when you see small bubbles on the side of the jar, though they can be hard to spot, depending on the vegetable. The best way to know when your pickles are ready is to give the jar a sniff and taste the vegetables. If the jar smells pleasantly sour, the cucumber has turned a dull green color, or the cabbage looks translucent, you're there. The fermented vegetables in Armenia are mild rather than deeply funky, and are often ready after 3 days of fermenting. Depending on your tastes, however, you may want to ferment for a week or more.

Salt-Brined Cucumber Pickles

Վարունգի թթու

Pickling cucumbers look like the cartoon version of cucumbers: They're slightly curved with bumps along their sides. Look for firm cucumbers that haven't yet started to wrinkle, preferably from a local market. Be sure to wash them, but don't use soap, which could remove any beneficial microbes that will help the vegetables ferment. For more notes on fermenting, refer to Small-Batch Pickles, page 131.

Makes 1 qt [960 ml]

> 1 lb [455 g] pickling cucumbers (about 5 cucumbers)
>
> 2 garlic cloves, peeled and halved
>
> 2 sprigs dill
>
> 2 cups [480 ml] water, plus more as needed
>
> 1½ Tbsp kosher salt, plus more as needed

Have a clean 1 qt [960 ml] widemouthed mason jar ready, with an airlock and a band to secure the airlock in place.

Trim the blossom end of the cucumbers (usually the dot on the narrower, darker end) to get rid of enzymes that cause cucumbers to soften as they ferment. Arrange as many cucumbers as you can to stand up in the container. Slice any remaining cucumbers in half and stack them on top of the whole cucumbers to fit in the jar, pressing them below the shoulder of the jar. Add the garlic and dill, pressing the ingredients along the sides of the jar.

In a liquid measuring cup, stir the water and salt together until the salt dissolves. Pour the brine over the cucumbers. (It's okay if you have extra. If you need more brine, mix ½ cup [120 ml] water with 1 tsp salt and pour it in.) Top the cucumbers with a few stacked lids or a resealable plastic bag filled with extra brine to keep them submerged. Place the airlock on top and secure it to the jar with the band.

Store in a cool area (between 60 and 75°F [15 and 24°C]) for 3 to 5 days, or until the cucumbers taste like pickles. By the third day, the brine will have turned cloudy and the cucumbers will look army-green. You may also see tiny bubbles rising to the top of the brine. Sediment may form at the base of the jar; that's perfectly okay. For a more sour pickle, let the cucumbers continue to ferment, checking them and burping the jar daily, for up to 2 weeks.

To store, replace the airlock with a regular lid and refrigerate the jar. The pickles keep, refrigerated, for up to 6 months.

Salt-Brined Mixed Pickles

Աղաջրի մեջ
պատրաստված
խառը թթու

The classic way to make this mixed pickle is by fermenting the vegetables together in a salt brine, but you can make a similar version using vinegar if time doesn't allow for fermenting. We're giving you both options here—this salt-brined version and a vinegar-brined version—so you can choose what works best for you. Before starting the salt-brined version, review Small-Batch Pickles, page 131.

Makes 1 qt [960 ml]

> 1 pickling cucumber, sliced diagonally into 1 in [2.5 cm] pieces
>
> ¼ small head green cabbage, cut into wedges 1 in [2.5 cm] thick (about 9 oz [260 g] total)
>
> 1 carrot, sliced diagonally into 2 in [5 cm] sticks
>
> 1 celery stick, cut diagonally into 2 in [5 cm] sticks
>
> 2 garlic cloves, smashed
>
> 2 sprigs dill
>
> 2 cups [480 ml] water, plus more as needed
>
> 1½ Tbsp kosher salt, plus more as needed

Have a clean 1 qt [960 ml] widemouthed mason jar ready, with an airlock and a band to secure the airlock in place.

Arrange the vegetables in any order so that they fit in the jar, wedging and pressing them under the shoulder of the jar. (You may have to use your best Tetris skills to get the vegetables to fit and a little force to crush the cabbage.) Add the garlic and dill, pressing the ingredients along the sides of the jar.

In a liquid measuring cup, stir the water and salt together until the salt dissolves. Pour the brine over the vegetables to cover completely. (It's okay if you have extra. If you need more brine, mix ½ cup [120 ml] water with 1 tsp salt and pour it in.) Top the vegetables with a few stacked lids or a plastic zip-top bag filled with extra brine to keep them submerged in the brine. Place the airlock on top and secure it to the jar with the band.

Store in a cool area (between 60 and 75°F [15 and 24°C]) for 5 to 7 days, or until the vegetables taste slightly sour. By the third day, the brine will have turned cloudy, and sediment may form at the base of the jar; that's perfectly okay.

To store, replace the airlock with a regular lid and refrigerate the jar. The pickles keep, refrigerated, for up to 6 months.

Vinegar-Brined Mixed Pickles

Քացախաջրի մեջ
պատրաստված խառը
թթու

This recipe uses the same vegetables as the salt-brined pickles, but it can be adjusted to add a spicy pepper or cauliflower in place of some of the cabbage. Essentially, the vegetables should add up to about 1 lb [455 g]. In this recipe, the salt is used to marinate the vegetables before they are pickled, and much of it is rinsed away before brining.

Makes 1 qt [960 ml]

1 pickling cucumber, sliced diagonally into 1 in [2.5 cm] pieces

¼ small head green cabbage, cut into wedges 1 in [2.5 cm] thick (about 9 oz [260 g] total)

1 carrot, sliced diagonally into 2 in [5 cm] sticks

1 celery stick, cut diagonally into 2 in [5 cm] sticks

1 Tbsp kosher salt

2 garlic cloves, smashed

2 sprigs dill

1 cup [240 ml] water

½ cup [120 ml] apple cider vinegar

Have a clean 1 qt [960 ml] widemouthed mason jar and lid (or similar-size heatproof container) ready.

Place the cucumber, cabbage, carrot, and celery in a colander and mix with the salt. Set aside for 1 hour, then rinse.

Arrange the vegetables in any order so that they fit in the jar, wedging and pressing them under the shoulder of the jar. (You may have to use your best Tetris skills to get the vegetables to fit and a little force to crush the cabbage.) Add the garlic and dill, pressing the ingredients along the sides of the jar.

In a small saucepan, bring the water and vinegar to a boil. Pour the brine over the vegetables, ensuring that there is enough liquid to cover them completely. Let cool to room temperature, then cover and refrigerate for a day or two before eating so the vegetables can soak up the brine. The pickles keep, refrigerated, for up to 6 months.

Pickled Green Peppers

Կանաչ պղպեղի թթու

Most of the peppers we encountered in Armenia were mild, green Hungarian peppers, but every once in a while, we'd get burned by a hot one. The most memorable time was while standing around a tonir chatting with lavash bakers. We sampled some of the pickled peppers the women had offered. One bite in, our eyes teared up and began to turn red—for a country that doesn't use hot sauce, this got us good. The women told us that it would be quite all right if we wished to throw the rest of the pepper into the tonir's fire. All this is to say that you can make these pickles with mild-mannered peppers, but feel free to throw in your favorite fiery variety to keep friends on their toes. Or sneak in a small dried red pepper for a milder spicy accent.

Makes 1 qt [960 ml]

1 lb [455 g] sweet greenish peppers, such as gypsy peppers, Hungarian sweet peppers, Anaheim peppers, or a mix

10 peppercorns

2 garlic cloves, peeled and halved

1¼ cups [300 ml] water

⅔ cup [160 ml] apple cider vinegar

1½ Tbsp granulated sugar

1 Tbsp kosher salt

-continued

Have a clean 1 qt [960 ml] widemouthed mason jar and lid (or similar-size heatproof container) ready.

Remove the cores and seeds from the peppers. Cut each pepper in half lengthwise if small, and skinny or in quarters lengthwise and crosswise if large (you want to be able to fit the pepper pieces into the jar).

Pack the peppers into the jar, starting with the larger, thicker pieces and ending with the smaller pieces. Add the peppercorns and garlic, pushing them in if necessary to position them lower in the jar.

In a medium saucepan, bring the water, vinegar, sugar, and salt to a boil. Pour the brine over the peppers, ensuring that there is enough liquid to cover the peppers completely to help preserve them. Let cool to room temperature, then cover and refrigerate for a day or two before eating so the pickles can soak up the brine. Pickled peppers keep in the refrigerator for up to 6 months.

Pickled Beets

Բազուկի թթու

Making use of the whole beet is common practice throughout Armenia—the greens are excellent in Jingalov Hats (page 58) and Beet Greens Soup (page 105). In fact, we're often tempted to load up on beets because we want the greens. That's okay, because we can always pickle what's left. Served with boiled potatoes, salty cheese, and fresh lavash, these beets are a perfect side to a simple lunch.

Makes 1 quart [960 ml]

1 lb [455 g] red beets, greens removed (about 3 beets)

1 garlic clove, peeled and halved

1 bay leaf

3 sprigs dill

1 cup [240 ml] water

½ cup [120 ml] apple cider vinegar

1 Tbsp granulated sugar

2 tsp kosher salt

Have a clean 1 qt [960 ml] mason jar and lid (or similar-size heatproof container) ready.

In a medium saucepan, cover the beets with water and bring to a boil. Lower to a gentle simmer, cover, and cook until the beets are tender when pierced with the tip of a knife, about 25 minutes. Drain.

When the beets are cool enough to handle, use your fingers or a paring knife to slip their skins off and discard. Cut the beets into quarters and pack into the jar. Add the garlic, bay leaf, and dill sprigs, pushing them in along the sides of the jar.

In a small saucepan, bring the water, vinegar, sugar, and salt to a boil. Pour the brine over the beets, ensuring that there is enough liquid to cover the beets completely to help preserve them. Let cool to room temperature, then cover and refrigerate for a day or two before eating so they can soak up the brine. Pickled beets keep in the refrigerator for up to 3 months.

Pickled Green Garlic

Կանաչ սխտորի թթու

Pickling green garlic in the spring is a classic Artsakh activity, where the end results are served as part of the pickle plate that accompanies nearly every meal. When packing garlic into jars, the trick is to place the bulbs in the base of the jar and the thin, dark green pieces at the top. This way, you eat the green parts first, because they absorb the brine the fastest.

Makes 2 packed cups [480 ml]

> **10 heads green garlic, with stalks (about 12 oz [340 g])**
>
> **5 black peppercorns**
>
> **2 juniper berries**
>
> **2 bay leaves**
>
> **3 sprigs flat-leaf parsley (optional)**
>
> **⅓ cup [80 ml] apple cider vinegar**
>
> **1 tsp kosher salt**
>
> **½ tsp granulated sugar (optional)**

Bring a pot of water to a boil. Have a clean 1 pt [480 ml] widemouthed mason jar and lid (or similar-size heatproof container) ready.

Trim the roots off the green garlic and ensure that they are thoroughly washed. Cut the bulb ends off and set aside. Cut the green garlic stalks into 2 in [5 cm] pieces. If the ends of the stalks are damaged or discolored, trim and discard the ends.

Add the bulbs to the water and cook for 2 minutes. Add the stalks and cook for 1 minute more. Set aside 1 cup [240 ml] of the cooking water, then drain the garlic pieces well. When cool enough to handle, separate the bulbs from the light green and dark green stalk pieces.

Pack the garlic into the jar, starting with the bulbs and continuing with the light green stalks, leaving the dark green stalks for the top. If you have too many dark green stalks to fit, leave them out (they can be sliced and mixed with roasted vegetables). Add the peppercorns, juniper berries, and bay leaves, using your fingers to push the seasonings deeper into the jar. Add the parsley sprigs on top, if there's room (this will depend on the size of the green garlic bulbs).

Mix ½ cup [240 ml] of the hot cooking water with the vinegar, salt, and sugar, if using, until the crystals have dissolved. Pour the mixture over the green garlic. If the pieces aren't submerged completely, top off with more of the hot cooking water. Secure the lid and give the jar a good shake to distribute the brine. Uncover the jar and let it cool completely on the counter. Then cover and refrigerate for a day or two before eating so the pickles can soak up the brine. The pickles keep, refrigerated, for 6 to 8 months.

Basturma

Բաստուրմա

cured beef in spices

The love for *basturma*, a lean, air-dried beef, is shared among Armenians all over the world. One of the best places to eat it is an outdoor spot called Basturma on Abovyan Street in the center of Yerevan. Jirair Avanian, who also owns Dolmama around the corner—one of Yerevan's first and still venerated fine-dining restaurants—got the idea right with this tiny location: You snack on the thinly sliced cured beef (pictured on facing page, left) flavored with garlic and *chemen* (fenugreek), as well as slices of Soujuk (page 142), a cured sausage (pictured on facing page, right), grab a glass of wine, and people watch. The next best way to enjoy basturma is to add slices of it to an omelet. Wrap the omelet in lavash and it's the Armenian equivalent of a breakfast burrito.

-continued

Makes about 2½ lb [1.2 kg]

While all meat-curing endeavors are projects, this one is simpler than most. First, salt the meat to draw out extra moisture. Next, coat it in the spice mixture and—here's the tricky part—hang it in a cool, airy place for a couple of days. (Ara also found he could do this step in the refrigerator; it just took longer.) You know it's done when it's firm enough to slice thinly with a sharp knife and the seasonings are infused into the meat. Before starting, read the instructions thoroughly to space the project over the course of several days and ensure you have room in the refrigerator. In Armenia, curing basturma is a project for cool, dry, fall weather. Likewise, we suggest undertaking this project when the climate is mild. If the indoor temperature is 70°F [21°C], expect the curing process to move faster than if it is chillier.

MEAT CURE

4 lb [1.8 kg] eye of round roast

1 lb [455 g] kosher salt

CHEMEN SEASONING MIX

½ cup [55 g] sweet paprika

½ cup [55 g] ground fenugreek

1 Tbsp ground allspice

1 Tbsp ground black pepper

2 tsp cayenne pepper

2 tsp ground cumin

1 tsp kosher salt

8 garlic cloves

1 cup [240 ml] water, plus more as needed

PART I: CURE THE MEAT

(3 Days)

To cure the meat, cut the eye of round roast in half crosswise so it's easier to work with. Each piece should be about 2 in [5 cm] thick. Using a skewer, poke the pieces all over (this will help the salt penetrate the meat).

Spread a thick layer of salt in a 9 by 13 in [23 by 33 cm] casserole or roasting pan and place the meat on top. Coat all sides of the meat with the salt so the meat is barely visible. Cover and refrigerate for 2 days.

After 2 days, the salt will have drawn out a lot of liquid from the meat. Fill a large bowl with cold water. Drain the meat and rinse off the salt. Submerge the meat in the cold water for at least 1 hour or up to 3 hours. (This will draw out any excess salt.)

Remove the meat from the water and thoroughly dry each piece with paper towels, pressing down to remove as much moisture as possible. Wrap the meat completely in paper towels and place on a half-sheet pan. Place another sheet pan on top of the meat. Weight down the pan with a few cans of tomatoes or something similar in weight and refrigerate overnight.

PART II: HANG THE MEAT

(5 to 10 Days)

Uncover the meat and remove the paper towels. The pieces should look flat and feel slightly firm.

Using a skewer like a needle and butcher's twine, pierce each piece about 1 in [2.5 cm] from the end and pull the twine through the hole. (You can pull it through by tying a knot on one end of the skewer and leaving the remaining thread long.) Find a place to tie up the meat to let it air-dry, preferably in a room with some airflow that never exceeds 70°F [21°C], for 5 to 10 days, or until the meat feels as firm as an avocado that's almost ripe. (Alternatively, hang the meat in the refrigerator for 8 to 14 days.) The meat should be dry from the curing process and won't drip at this point.

PART III: ADD THE CHEMEN SEASONING MIX

(3 to 5 Days)

Untie the meat (but leave the string in place) and move it onto a half-sheet pan.

To prepare the seasoning mix, in a medium bowl, mix together the paprika, fenugreek, allspice, black pepper, cayenne, cumin, and salt. In a food processor (preferably a mini one), puree the garlic with ½ cup [120 ml] of the water. Add the garlic puree to the bowl of spices and mix thoroughly. Pour in the remaining ½ cup [120 ml] of water, or more if needed, until it resembles thick pancake batter.

Smear the spice mixture all over the meat in a thin but even layer about ⅛ in [4 mm] thick. You should not be able to see the meat. Rehang the meat for 2 to 3 more days (or 3 to 5 days in a refrigerator) or until the spice mixture has firmed up and is dry to the touch. At this point, the basturma is ready to eat. To serve, slice as thinly as possible with a sharp knife. Keep it wrapped tightly in plastic wrap in the refrigerator for up to 3 months.

Soujuk

Սուջուկ

dry-cured sausage

It's hard to talk about Basturma (page 138) without also mentioning *soujuk* (pictured on page 139, right), a dry-cured sausage that is often served right alongside the spice-coated cured beef. The two can also be interchangeable: Basturma with Eggs (page 122) can just as easily be soujuk with eggs. There are a range of ways to make this traditional sausage—we've read recipes in which ground meat is packed into stockings before being strung up to dry and others that recommend sewing together fabric to create sausage casings. For this version, Ara developed a sausage with the flavor and appearance of soujuk while incorporating more modern techniques of making dry-cured sausages.

Makes eight 12 in [30 cm] sausages

We're including this recipe because it is such an iconic cured meat in Armenia (and among diaspora communities). The caveat is this is not a beginner recipe, and it can take a month to make from start to finish. It will also occupy room in a refrigerator through the curing process, so it is easiest to do this when you have room to spare in there. If you've never cured meat before, start by making basturma. When you're ready to move to soujuk, invite a friend with sausage-making experience (and equipment) over to lend a hand. For equipment, have a 5 lb [2.3 kg] sausage press handy and either a sausage prick or a sewing needle. (Although KitchenAid mixers have a sausage-stuffing contraption that attaches to its meat grinder, it is tricky to use for this recipe and we recommend seeking out a sausage press instead.) You will also need a couple of specific ingredients. Pink curing salt #2 (also called Prague powder #2), which is made by several brands, ensures that the meat stays free of harmful bacteria as it ages. Natural hog casing is sold a couple of ways, but Ara uses dry-salted, tubed casings, which are easier to use. Finally, Bactroferm T-spx is a starter culture that encourages a slow, mild acidification of the sausage, improving flavor while also lowering the pH level to ensure the sausage is safe to eat. Look for supplies on sausagemaker.com. A final note: To ensure accuracy, the ingredient quantities are all in both weight and volume measurements. We suggest defaulting to gram measurements when possible.

9 ft [2.75 m] salted natural hog casing

¼ tsp [0.25 g] Bactroferm T-spx (starter culture)

2 Tbsp [28 g] distilled water or water that has been boiled and cooled to room temperature

1 Tbsp [10 g] sweet paprika

1 Tbsp [10 g] garlic powder

1 tsp [5 g] ground allspice

1 tsp [5 g] ground cumin

1¾ oz [50 g] kosher salt

¼ oz [8 g] pink curing salt #2

4 lb [1.8 kg] ground beef (preferably with an 85/15 meat-to-fat ratio), chilled thoroughly

PART I: STUFF AND PRESS THE SAUSAGES

(4 to 5 days)

The day before making the sausage, rinse all the salt off the casing, being sure to flush the insides out as well. Let the casing soak in a bowl of cold water overnight in the refrigerator.

The next day, place a mixing bowl large enough to hold the meat in the refrigerator. In a small bowl, combine the Bactroferm and water. Stir them together and let the culture bloom for 5 to 10 minutes.

In another small bowl, mix together the paprika, garlic powder, allspice, cumin, kosher salt, and pink curing salt.

Place the meat in the large chilled bowl and sprinkle evenly with the seasoning mix. With clean hands, thoroughly mix the spices into the meat. To keep the meat as cold as possible,

-continued

work quickly and avoid overhandling the meat. Drizzle the starter culture and water over the meat and continue to knead the meat until it becomes tacky and begins to stick to your fingers, 2 to 3 minutes. Place the bowl in the refrigerator and let the meat rest and re-chill for at least 30 minutes or up to 4 hours.

Set up a sausage press and drain the casing. Clear a large space on the counter and have a cutting board and a roll of paper towels handy.

Add the meat mixture to the bowl of a sausage press. Slide the entire length of the casing onto the nozzle of the press by scrunching it up like a tight accordion. If all of the casing doesn't fit, cut it in half and fill the casing in two batches. To start, crack the press just until the first of the meat comes to the end of the nozzle, then tie the end of the casing in a knot in front of the nozzle. Slowly crank the press with one hand while holding the end of the nozzle and moving your hand back and forth along the nozzle to guide the casing as the meat fills in. (This is easier to do with two people; one cranking the press and one filling the casing.) Avoid air pockets by working slowly but also avoid filling the casing so tightly that it splits. If the casing breaks, just cut the casing at the tear, tie a knot at the end, and start a new link.

Once all the meat is in the casing, begin to portion the size of the soujuk by pinching the casing together every 2 ft [61 cm] and twisting it three or four times. Once you have twisted all the soujuk links, snip each twist with sharp kitchen shears so you have individual portions.

(The twisted casing will keep the sausage filling in place.) Bend each portion so the sausage is folded in half (this will make it easier to hang later). Prick the folded soujuk all over with a sausage prick or a needle to get as many air pockets out as you can.

Put a layer of paper towels on a cutting board and lay the folded soujuk on top in one layer. You should have four folded sausages. Cover with another sheet of paper towels. Lay a half-sheet pan on top of the sausages and press it down. You want to flatten out the sausage to about ½ in [12 mm] thick. Then weight down the pan with a few cans of tomatoes or something similar in weight and store in a cool, dry place for 2 days. Do not let the temperature exceed 70°F [21°C].

PART II: HANG THE SAUSAGES

(3 to 4 weeks)

Remove the weights and the sheet pan. At this point, the soujuk will be evenly flattened and the casings will be slightly dry. Tie a loop of butcher's twine around the bend of the soujuk. Get creative and rig a rack in the refrigerator that will let you hang the soujuk with the help of the butcher's twine (you can prop a honing steel against a shelf, for instance). Hang the soujuk in the refrigerator for 3 to 4 weeks, or until the soujuk is dark reddish-purple throughout and feels as firm as dry-aged salami. Soujuk keeps in a zip-top plastic bag for up to 3 months in the refrigerator.

Yerevan

On a sunny afternoon on Saryan Street in April 2018, we started to hear the kind of commotion you'd expect when a country wins the World Cup. A twentysomething Yerevantsi standing in front of In Vino, a wine bar, looked up from his phone. He gave his friend a bear hug. Three girls sitting at a sidewalk table simultaneously began to laugh and cry. Soon every driver was tapping a celebratory pa-pa-papapa on the horn.

"What happened?" we asked as we walk into In Vino. Mariam Saghatelyan, one of the partners at the wine bar, turned up the radio to hear the news over the horns in the street.

"The prime minister resigned and they've released Nikol." In shock, she brought out a sparkling wine from Takar, a local producer. The wine tasted lean with a saline funk. "Bubbles for Nikol!" we cheered. Armenia might never be the same.

We were visiting Armenia during a pivotal time in the country's modern history. In 2015, as a way to circumvent term limits, the governing Republican party of Armenia altered the country's constitution, transferring power from a president elected by the people to a prime minister voted on by Parliament. This allowed Parliament to put President Serzh Sargsyan back into power as prime minister after term limits forced him to step down as president. The incident sparked protests across the country, the majority of which were led by Nikol Pashinyan. A former jailed journalist turned politician, Pashinyan

began walking across the Armenian countryside, drawing crowds of supporters along the way as he talked to them about the changes they wanted to see in their country. By the time he reached Yerevan, protests blocked traffic to make way for him while chants of "Nikol! Nikol!" filled the air. Pashinyan's slogan, duc hov, a Russian-Armenian phrase meaning "be brave" or "with spirit," was plastered on posters, hats, and T-shirts.

The day before we stepped into In Vino, Pashinyan had been put in prison, a last attempt by the government to stifle the opposition, but which only made the protests grow larger and louder. John had a front-row seat to the arrest, which resulted in him getting hit with a concussion grenade set off by the police to disperse the crowd of protestors. (It also resulted in a visit to the hospital for stitches in his leg.) When news of Pashinyan's release got out, the protesters turned into partiers, and we joined in, toasting to a new Armenia with Mariam while celebrations broke out across the city. At that moment, Yerevan became the center of Armenia's Velvet Revolution. By the time we left the city in May 2018, Pashinyan had been voted in as prime minister, and it felt as if Armenia was on the brink of changing its corrupt government for good.

That Yerevan holds such an important place in Armenian society is a relatively new occurrence. The ancient city of Erebuni precedes the founding of the Roman Empire, but in the early twentieth century, it was a hodgepodge town of narrow roads lined with walled gardens and dense markets crowded with coffee stalls. It probably had the feeling of a trading post on the edge of the Orient, and in a way, it

-continued

had been: For a few centuries, Yerevan had been part of both the Persian and the Russian empires. By the turn of the twentieth century, the city had 28,000 residents, a mix of Armenians, Russians, and Muslims from various backgrounds. It was only after Armenians escaping genocide migrated to the city that it was remade primarily as an Armenian city. By the 1930s, it was completely rebuilt according to Soviet requirements.

For the past five years, though, Yerevan, or at least the city center, has adopted the feeling of a European city filled with cafés, wine bars, and restaurants. The changes began in 2012 when In Vino opened as a wine shop and bar, promoting a culture of drinking wine. The shop brought in bottles from Italy and Armenia to educate palates and reconnect people with the country's ancient winemaking roots. Its success prompted other wine bars to pop up along Saryan Street, turning a once-sleepy road into one of the first places to go for a thirst-quenching stroll.

As Saryan Street took off, spurring wine bars and Wi-Fi–enabled outdoor cafés to open across the center of the city, it was easy to forget about Soviet times altogether, which is why a meal at Gayanei Mot ("At Gayane's") felt like stepping back in time. Getting to Gayane's required walking through an archway and into an apartment complex courtyard where a small sign in the corner read "restaurant." In a Soviet-era dining room, Gayane Areyshatyan played the piano while we dined on khashlama and tolma, toasting friends with mulberry vodka. While Gayane has since passed, we hope her warm style of hospitality lives on.

Before we left Yerevan that May, we witnessed another all-day (and night) street party as Yerevantsis celebrated a fresh start with Pashinyan voted in as prime minister. At In Vino, Mariam had a new bottle of rosé waiting for us. This time, the label simply said "duc hov."

Feasting

Khash, Khorovats, and
Heartier Dishes

he stairs of most Soviet-era apartment buildings we encountered were dark, making them hard to navigate for unaccustomed Americans. But as soon as our hosts would open the door, we'd forget about feeling lost and enter a welcoming space centered around a table filled with food. While the rest of the meal was being prepared—Summer Tolma (page 178) when the weather was hot, Khashlama (page 208) when it was colder—we passed the time by snacking on salt-brined pickles and eating salty cheese wrapped in lavash with cilantro, dill, and skinny green onions.

We encountered this scene over and over again in Armenia, and each meal contributed recipes that we sought to re-create in this chapter, which begins with Khash (page 156), a type of bone broth that is legendary on its own, not necessarily for its flavor but for the ritual behind eating it. A *khash* party is a category all its own, an all-day affair that starts in the morning with bowls of the hot, rich broth and vodka to help with digestion—or so we're told.

After that, we move on to one of the most enjoyable ways to celebrate good weather and friendship—*khorovats*. The Armenian answer to grilling is familiar but also has a few twists, such as using long, sturdy skewers instead of grill grates to cook meat and vegetables. When making khorovats, the method is more important than any single recipe, so we provide an overview of the process and an all-purpose seasoning rub to make it easier to mix and match.

The remainder of the chapter digs deeper into feasting options, from the aforementioned stuffed vegetable tolma to Lavash-Wrapped Trout baked until crisp (page 183), a different form of *kufta* baked in lavash (page 189), and comforting porridges and stews. Every dish in this chapter is at its best when served with an herb and cheese plate (see page 35), a side of bread, and a salad or side (or both) from the previous chapter.

There is also an important part of feasting that goes beyond food. The Caucasus are famous for their long history of toasting rituals, and it's possible that these rituals go back more than 6,000 years, when the world's first-known wineries appeared. In the past two centuries, Russian influences replaced wine with vodka and brandy, but the desire to commemorate a gathering with a series of toasts continued.

Often, a toastmaster—a *tamadan*—leads the toast. If you're at someone's home, this is typically the master of the house, nearly always a man. While the tamadan is toasting, it's rude to interrupt or eat. After the toast is made, everyone clinks glasses and downs the vodka, and then the tamadan refills the glasses so guests will be ready for the next toast.

Glasses of Kompot (page 221) may also be filled to sip after the vodka.

One of the most important ritualized toasts happens while eating khash. The toasts may go something like this:

> The inaugural toast: "Good morning!" (A khash party starts well before lunch.)
>
> The second toast: "So we don't forget the first toast."
>
> The third toast: "To the maker of the khash."
>
> The fourth toast: "To the eaters of the khash."
>
> The final toast: "To the next khash."

But toasting can also take place at a gathering of khorovats, a meal shared over harissa, or any time a group of people have come together to share a meal. One of our favorite toasts on our research trips was "to new friends," because we met so many on the road.

Not every toasting opportunity needs to be structured, however, and nowadays guests may simply clink glasses and say *"kenats"* ("to life"), just as if they were to say "cheers."

Khash

խ ш с

all-day bone broth

The easiest way to describe *khash* is that it's a rich broth made of calves' feet. But the real answer is more of a social ritual involving at least four people that starts at the crack of dawn (or no later than 9 a.m.) and lasts through several toasts—and vodka shots—before ideally leading to a nap. The day typically ends with Armenian coffee and sweets—and a plan for the next khash party.

Not too long ago, khash parties were for men only (the hangover cure of champions), but the events have become a lot more inclusive in recent years. The best time of the year for khash events is late fall and winter. By November, Yerevan's GUM market is ready with khash party supplies, the sidewalk lined with tables holding impeccably white calves feet, the hoof ends neatly pointed toward the customers. Inside, stacks of lavash rolled into tubes and dried are sold for the specific purpose of crumbling into the broth to thicken it. If the season for khash in Yerevan is over, those who need their fix can head into the snow-capped mountains. One summer, Ara and his family went by taxi to Mount Aragats, a volcanic peak northwest of Yerevan, to eat khash. After inviting the driver to join them, they sat beside a clear alpine lake, sopping up the broth with lavash.

-continued

Serves 8

In California, Ara makes khash not only for parties but also to recover from triathlons. With all the collagen in the broth, it has to have some sort of restorative properties. Calves' feet, which give the broth its rich body, can be found at Middle Eastern or kosher butcher shops, as well as at Asian markets. Ara likes to add onion and garlic to the broth for flavor, but in Armenia the broth is made solely with the bones and water. When throwing a khash party, have both dried and fresh lavash at the table so everyone can customize their bowl, crumbling dried lavash into the broth to thicken it while draping fresh lavash over the bowl to keep it "cozy." So you may want more lavash at the table than is called for in this recipe. Everything else on the table—the minced garlic, salt, lemon wedges, and herb and cheese plate—is all there to enhance the khash experience. (Ara also offers Aleppo pepper at the table.) And there is always vodka to help with digestion. "You cannot eat khash without vodka," the saying goes, "they are like brothers."

BROTH

4 lb [1.8 kg] calves' feet, each foot cut into 3 to 6 pieces

1 yellow onion, quartered

4 garlic cloves, peeled but kept whole

TO SERVE

8 sheets homemade Lavash (page 48) or 4 sheets store-bought lavash

1 head garlic, broken into cloves and peeled

½ tsp kosher salt, plus more for seasoning

3 lemons, cut into wedges

DAY ONE To make the broth, place the feet in a 12 qt [12 L] stockpot and cover with cold water. Refrigerate for 4 hours or up to 2 days, changing the water once or twice. This allows the meat to soften and removes any impurities, resulting in a cleaner-tasting broth.

Drain the water and rinse the feet. Return the feet to the pot and cover with about 2 in [5 cm] of water. Add the onion and garlic cloves. Bring the pot to a boil, then partially cover and lower to a gentle simmer. Cook for 5 hours, checking the water level occasionally to ensure the bones are always covered. The broth will have a yellow tint from the fat; using a ladle, skim as much of the fat from the top as you can. When the broth is ready, the meat should feel tender when pierced with a fork and slide off easily from the bone. You can also test to see if the broth is done by dipping a finger (if you are tolerant to heat) or the spoon into the broth and then pressing your fingers together or holding the spoon against a plate. If the broth feels sticky, it is ready. If not, cover and continue to simmer for 1 hour more and test again (the broth should not take more than 8 hours).

Let the broth cool with the onion, garlic, and meat in it. At this point, the broth can be refrigerated overnight.

Cut the lavash pieces in half. Keep half of them in a plastic bag to prevent them from drying out. (If they feel dry, mist them with a little water, wrap them in a kitchen towel, and let them soften.) Leave the remaining lavash uncovered at room temperature to dry. This can be done overnight. If the lavash isn't crisp, toast the pieces in an oven heated to 350°F [180°C] for 6 to 8 minutes. This lavash will be used to crumble into the broth to thicken it.

DAY TWO When the broth is completely cold, a layer of yellow fat will have risen to the top. Use a spoon to scrape off and remove the fat from the top. Pull out the large bones, leaving the meat behind, and bring the broth to a simmer.

Before serving, place the peeled garlic cloves in a mini food processor and blend with the salt. (This step takes away some of the raw bite of the garlic, but it is optional; you can also serve the garlic minced without the salt.) Transfer the garlic to a bowl and set on the table along with the remaining ingredients for serving.

To serve, divide a couple of pieces of meat into each bowl and spoon the hot broth on top. Advise guests to add 1 tsp of garlic, a squeeze of lemon, and a generous pinch of salt before tasting. From there, they can season it more as they please.

Before eating, crush dried lavash directly over the bowl and mix it into the broth, and offer fresh lavash alongside for dipping. If you're so inclined, pour your guests small shots of vodka.

Khorovats
ARMENIAN GRILLING

While grilling meat on skewers is common around the world, the act is taken on with rare passion in Armenia. The celebratory nature of khorovats was on full display on May 8, 2018, when the country's Velvet Revolution culminated in the election of Nikol Pashinyan as prime minister. Traffic stopped in Yerevan to make room for a citywide party, and revelers dragged their charcoal-fueled mangals into the streets, dancing with skewers of meat pointing at the sky. That's what makes khorovats easy to like: the equipment is mobile, the preparation is simple, and the chargrilled results can fuel a party.

It doesn't take a revolution to go all-in on a khorovats feast, though. Something as simple as good weather and an opportunity to get together with family and friends can be reason enough to celebrate.

For those unacquainted with the term khorovats, think of shish kebab, except that instead of meat and vegetables threaded onto the same skewer, the two are cooked separately to ensure both are evenly cooked. The biggest difference between a mangal (a khorovats-style grill) and an American grill is the lack of grates; cooks prop long skewers of meat and vegetables over either side of the mangal, suspending the meat and vegetables directly over the embers without worrying that some pieces will stick to the grill.

Some styles of khorovats are also cooked in a tonir, picking up the smoke left from the embers of the fire that fueled a lavash-baking session. But the more direct connection between khorovats and lavash is that the flatbread is simply practical to have on hand. Wrap a sheet around the meat and tug on the skewer until you unsheathe it like a sword.

We learned about the nuances of khorovats during a conversation with Armen Qefilyan, a chef in the northern town of Alaverdi. Qefilyan took home first place in a national khorovats competition in 2009, a victory that allowed him to grow his business. He now operates two restaurants catering to tourists visiting UNESCO World Heritage monasteries along the Debed Gorge. To Armen, there might as well be a metaphorical Debed Gorge separating the act of dragging a mangal into the street and how he prepares championship-worthy khorovats. Compared with most of the khorovats we saw, where flames licked the meat as it cooked, Armen favors a gentle fire, one that allows him to hold his hand over the coals and count to twelve. For his winning entry in the competition, he seasoned lamb with salt, paprika, black pepper, dried thyme, and dried savory, and threaded the meat onto skewers with lamb tail fat in between the pieces to enhance richness. To present his entry to the judges, he placed the lamb on a sheet of lavash and scattered pomegranate seeds on top.

Armen's low-and-slow khorovats technique yields not only exquisite lamb but also tender pork chops, which we ate under a tree at his namesake restaurant, Armen's. Yet there is a place for flame-licked char in khorovats cooking. In Stepanakert, we stepped into a local police hangout and ordered pork khorovats, watching as the cook threw branches into the corner of the stone mangal, causing the flames to crawl up its sides. Our chops, which came bundled in lavash with sliced onions and herbs, were charred in parts, but they were also salty and juicy—and so memorable we wished we could have returned for more. Taking these two extremes into consideration, we opt for the middle ground, somewhere between a gentle and roaring fire, which gives more room for whatever is on the menu that day.

With a bit of prep and our guide on page 162, you'll be grilling like a champion in no time.

A Guide to Khorovats

Before you start, go over options for setting up a grill and then make a seasoning rub. With the following guidelines, you'll be able to scale up or down the amount of food you prepare, depending on how many people you're feeding.

1. CONFIGURE YOUR GRILL

Mangals are rectangular boxes made of steel; they run about 6 to 8 in [15 to 20 cm] deep and 12 to 18 in [30.5 to 46 cm] wide, and can be anywhere from 2 to 10 ft [0.6 to 3 m] long. The length isn't the important part, though; it's the width that matters. Because a mangal does not have grill grates, the skewers need to act like grates. You get this effect by propping the skewers across the mangal like rungs on a ladder.

Before you start, ensure you have **skewers** that fit comfortably crosswise on your mangal. In Armenia, they're called *shampoors*, but elsewhere they go by other names, such as *shashlik* skewers or kebab skewers. The most important thing is that they are long, metal, and either flat or beveled but never round (this allows the meat to stay snugly in place as you rotate the skewers). Search for "mangal" online and chances are you'll be directed to some appropriate skewers.

If you're all set with skewers but short a mangal, make one out of a classic round **Weber grill**. Simply remove the grill grate and make sure your skewers are at least the diameter of the Weber. Place one skewer across one side of the mouth of the grill and one skewer across the other side of the grill to make a rectangle. This will hold your skewers and allow you to rotate your skewers without burning your hands. If your skewers aren't long enough but you have an old barbecue chimney starter, try to place it upside down in the center of the Weber and scatter the charcoal pieces around it. Then you can prop the skewers over the grill like spokes on a bicycle.

And if you don't have a Weber grill but are out camping or having a picnic, configure a mangal with a large, deep aluminum foil roasting pan. Just place coals on the bottom and start them up, lay skewers right on top, and you'll have a super-makeshift, disposable mangal.

If you're working with a **gas grill**, see if the skewers are long enough to fit across the grill without falling in. Or try to remove half of the grates. On the open section, lay a fish basket across the grill and use it as a way to prop the ends of the skewers on one side so they don't fall in.

If you can't do without the grates, just ensure that the grill grates you are using are very clean and lightly oiled to prevent meat and vegetables from sticking.

2. MARINATE AND SKEWER THE MEAT

We took a cue from Armen Qefilyan and kept the seasonings simple, allowing the quality of the meat to shine through and the fire to do the rest of the work.

Seasoning Rub

Makes enough for 20 lb [9 kg] of meat or fish, about 6 khorovats parties

   ½ cup [85 g] kosher salt

   ¼ cup [28 g] dried thyme

   ¼ cup [28 g] dried savory
   (preferably summer savory)

   3 Tbsp ground black pepper

   3 Tbsp sweet paprika

Mix all the ingredients together and store indefinitely in an airtight container at room temperature.

For every 1 lb [455 g] of **meat or fish**, marinate with 2 tsp of **Seasoning Rub** and one-quarter of a **thinly sliced yellow onion**.

3. PICK A PROTEIN

Beef tenderloin, rib eye, pork loin, pork tenderloin, pork riblets, leg of lamb, lamb chops, whole trout—you get it, the choices are endless. The one thing that stays constant is the size of the cubes used for khorovats.

With the exception of chops and whole trout, the meat is best when cut into cubes of similar size so they cook evenly. Generally speaking, plan on **3 lbs [1.4 kg] of boneless lamb, pork, steak, or chicken thighs** for six to eight people. In Armenia, you never want to be short on meat in case that party of six unexpectedly increases to a party of ten. Plus, leftovers make good sandwiches smashed between pieces of Matnakash (page 68).

FOR BONELESS MEAT: Cut the meat into 1½ to 2 in [4 to 5 cm] cubes. In a large bowl, mix the meat well with the Seasoning Rub and **one-quarter of yellow onion** per lb [455 g]. Refrigerate for at least 2 hours or overnight. Thread the pieces of meat onto skewers straight through the center of each cube, so that the pieces touch each other (but are not squished together). Leave enough metal exposed at the ends so the skewer can be propped onto the edges of the grill.

FOR BONE-IN MEAT: Marinate the meat the same way as the cubed meat, but ensure the bone runs alongside the skewer when skewering the meat. Lamb and pork chops can be skewered this way. Depending on the size of the cuts, two large chops and three to four small chops can fit on one skewer.

For trout, use the same amount of seasonings to marinate the fish but shorten the marinating time to 30 minutes. Skewer the fish from the mouth to the tail so the skewer runs parallel with the backbone, and use one large skewer per fish.

4. COOK THE PROTEIN

Keeping an eye out for all the variables, such as the heat, the type of grill, and the meat itself, is all part of the fun and experience of khorovats.

START THE FIRE: One of the keys to good khorovats is hot coals. Any lump hardwood, such as mesquite, oak, or even grapevine, will work. If you have a chimney starter, start the coals in it by crumpling up newspaper into balls at the base and then placing the lump hardwood on top, using pieces of different sizes to enhance the fire-catching abilities of the chimney. Light the paper at the base of the chimney and let it burn until the coals start to catch fire and glow. Using a grill mitt, lift the chimney by the handle out of the grill. Then pile the coals back up with grill tongs, adding a little more charcoal to keep the fire going. Let the coals burn until gray and covered in ash, with no black showing, then spread them out across the grill for even, direct-heat cooking.

TEMPERATURE CHECK: When you can hold your hand over where you're placing the skewers for no more than 5 seconds, the fire is ready to go for quick-cooking, tender cuts of meat and any kind of fish. For tougher cuts of meat that benefit from slower cooking times, opt for a flame that's slightly cooler and allows you to hold your hand over the coals for 6 to 7 seconds. Keep an eye on the charcoal as you work, adding more to fuel the fire if the coals start to cool before you're ready to call it a day.

START GRILLING: While cooking, rotate the skewers often and keep them near the center of the grill where it's hotter. Flare-ups happen when rich cuts of meat drip fat into the coals, and they can add a nice char, but they should be few and far between. If you have too many flare-ups, move the affected skewer to a cooler part of the grill.

For tender boneless cuts, such as beef tenderloin, rib eye, pork loin, pork tenderloin, and

tender bone-in cuts, like lamb chops, cook for 3 to 5 minutes per side or until nicely golden brown, with a bit of char in places.

For tougher cuts of meat, like pork ribs, beef ribs, and leg of lamb, cook for at least 10 to 15 minutes per side, rotating often. Calculate longer cooking times for bone-in chicken pieces, too.

5. SERVE UP THE KHOROVATS

Have a large bowl with **a thinly sliced yellow onion** ready so that when the meat comes off the grill, you can pull the meat off the skewer with tongs directly into the bowl. Give it a good mix so that the juices mingle with the onion and then sprinkle some **chopped flat-leaf parsley**, **cilantro**, and **dill** over the top (a handful of each chopped herb will do the trick).

6. REMEMBER THE VEGETABLES

While the grill is going, grill vegetables, too. In Shushi, an ancient fortress city outside of Stepanakert, Saro Saryan runs a guesthouse where he feeds visitors with khorovats, including **potatoes threaded onto skewers interspersed with pieces of pork fat**. Smoky and rich, they were a highlight of the feast. Options for vegetables include **Anaheim or Hungarian peppers**, **whole tomatoes**, **whole eggplant**, and either **whole or sliced potatoes**.

For all vegetables, coat them in a little **oil** and season with a little **salt and pepper**—the grill will do the rest of the seasoning. Consider

grilling vegetables like eggplants and tomatoes before the meat because they can be served at room temperature (or turned into Khorovats Salad, page 167).

GRILLED EGGPLANT: Use **1 long, slender eggplant**, such as Italian eggplant, for two or three people. Cut off the stem ends and then skewer the eggplant from end to end. (If they are small, you may be able to fit 2 on each skewer.) Coat with a little **oil** and season with **salt**. Cook the eggplants, rotating every 5 to 10 minutes, until they are tender all the way through, with the skin mostly charred in places but not completely black, 15 to 20 minutes. Slide the eggplants off the skewers. To serve, split open each eggplant and season with **salt**, **pepper**, a little **oil**, and chopped **herbs**, such as **cilantro, flat-leaf parsley, and dill**.

GRILLED TOMATOES: Pick **1 sturdy ripe tomato** per person. Trim the stem ends and thread them onto the skewer from end to end. Coat with a little **oil** and season with **salt**. Cook the tomatoes, rotating once, until the skin begins to blister and turn black, 4 to 6 minutes. Slide the tomatoes off the skewer and season with **salt and pepper**.

GRILLED POTATOES: Pick **1 Yukon gold potato or 2 fingerling potatoes** per person. If using Yukon golds, slice them crosswise into 1 in [2.5 cm] rounds. If using fingerlings, slice off the tips of each potato. Coat the potatoes with a little **oil** and season with **salt and pepper**. Use your hands to rub the oil and seasonings over

the potatoes evenly. Spear the Yukon gold slices crosswise at a slight diagonal, ensuring there is space between each piece to encourage even cooking. Spear the fingerling potatoes from end to end. Grill, rotating the skewers every 5 to 10 minutes, until the potatoes are tender when pierced with a knife, about 20 minutes.

7. REMEMBER THE LAVASH

You can also use a hot grill to cook up sheets of **lavash** for a khorovats feast. The difference is that you'll need grill grates or a way to prop a large (two-burner) cast-iron griddle across the grill. It's also best to cook lavash before anything else so the coals are at their hottest. For more on grilling lavash, see page 53. If you aren't planning on making lavash, buy some to have handy for eating with khorovats.

8. USE THE OVEN

If it rains on your khorovats parade, take the party inside and make use of the oven and its broiler setting. This is where casserole-friendly Urfa Kebab (page 169) can save the day.

Khorovats Salad

Խորոված քանչարեղենի աղցան

grilled eggplant and tomato salad

When preparing khorovats, a standard practice is to also grill skewers of tomatoes and eggplants, which are served at room temperature, peeled but otherwise unadorned. This recipe takes the same idea of that simple side, but seasons the vegetables like a salad, with onion, herbs, and a little oil and lemon juice. It's a dish we fell hard for at a khorovats party in California with the Sargsyan family; the mild smokiness of the vegetables in a tart, garlicky salad is the perfect complement for grilled meat.

-continued

Serves 4 to 6

To prepare on the grill, skewer the eggplants from stem to end, squeezing 2 onto a skewer if the skewers are long enough. Alternatively, you can use the oven to roast the eggplants until charred on the outside and soft in the center and broil the tomatoes. If you do it this way, you can prepare it well in advance of firing up the grill, freeing up more time to focus on the grilling.

2 largish slender eggplants, such as Italian or Japanese (about 2 lb [910 g] total)

2 Tbsp sunflower oil or other neutral oil, plus more for coating the vegetables

4 sturdy tomatoes, such as Romas

¼ yellow onion, thinly sliced

3 green onions, thinly sliced

2 garlic cloves, minced

2 Tbsp lemon juice

1 tsp kosher salt

¼ tsp crushed dried red pepper

2 Tbsp chopped dill

½ cup [20 g] chopped cilantro

If grilling, prepare a grill for direct-heat cooking (see Start the Fire, page 163). Cut the tops off the eggplants. Skewer from end to end, using separate skewers for each one if they do not fit on a single skewer. Rub lightly with oil and repeat with the tomatoes. (If using round tomatoes instead of Romas, skewer the tomatoes from side to side, with the stem ends facing up.) Grill, rotating often, until the insides of the vegetables are soft but not falling apart, about 5 minutes for the tomatoes and 20 minutes for the eggplants

(resist the urge to char the outsides of the eggplants completely).

Set aside until cool enough to handle, then peel and discard the skins while still warm.

If roasting in the oven, preheat the broiler. Put the eggplants and tomatoes on a half-sheet pan and lightly coat with oil. Broil the vegetables for 3 to 5 minutes or until they start to char on the top. Turn the oven to 500°F [260°C] and roast the vegetables, rotating occasionally with tongs, until they are completely soft and slightly charred, about 15 minutes for the tomatoes and 25 minutes for the eggplants. Set aside until cool enough to handle, then peel and discard the skins.

Soak the onion and green onions in cold water for 5 minutes to take away their raw bite. Drain.

Dice the cooked eggplants and tomatoes and transfer to a large serving bowl. (They will not hold their shape, and that's perfectly okay.) Mix in the onion, green onion, 2 Tbsp of oil, garlic, lemon juice, salt, and red pepper flakes. Taste, adding more salt or pepper if needed. Mix in most of the herbs, leaving some to sprinkle on top as a garnish before serving. Serve at room temperature.

Urfa Kebab

Ուրֆա կյաբաբ

skewers of eggplant and meatballs

Urfa, once an important city in Western Armenia, may have been the origin of this recipe composed of meatballs threaded on skewers with eggplant. This oven-ready dish takes the idea of khorovats and transfers it inside. For a variation, you can thread slices of tomatoes in between the meat and eggplants, which is how Ara grew up eating it.

-continued

Serves 4 to 6

A popular summer vegetable in Armenia, eggplants are especially good when they get a little char. In this recipe, we use the broiler to capture that effect, though if you have a grill going for khorovats, consider grilling the skewers briefly just for flavor before putting them in the oven to bake. (If grilling, soak the wooden skewers ahead of time to prevent them from burning.) The key here is to get skinny, long eggplants, such as Italian or Japanese varieties. Globe eggplant is too round for this preparation.

1½ lb [680 g] ground beef (preferably with an 80/20 meat-to-fat ratio)

½ yellow onion, finely diced

2 tsp kosher salt, plus more for seasoning

¼ tsp ground black pepper

¼ tsp ground allspice

¼ tsp crushed dried red pepper

4 smallish Japanese or Italian eggplants (about 1 lb [455 g] total)

1 Tbsp sunflower or other neutral oil

Preheat the oven to 350°F [180°C]. Lightly oil a roasting pan or half-sheet pan. Have 6 wooden skewers ready.

In a large mixing bowl, combine the beef, onion, 1½ tsp of salt, the pepper, allspice, and red pepper. Continue to mix the meat for a few minutes until the spices are evenly blended and the meat feels tacky.

Slice the eggplants crosswise into 24 pieces about 1 in [2.5 cm] thick. Season with ¼ tsp salt and lightly coat with the oil.

Roll the meat into 18 pieces about the size of large golf balls. In alternating layers, starting and ending with the eggplant, thread the eggplant rounds and meatballs onto the skewers so that the pieces fit snugly, using 3 meatballs and 4 eggplant pieces per skewer. Press down gently on the meatballs so they are the same thickness as the eggplant rounds.

Place the skewers in the pan and season the tops with the remaining ¼ tsp salt. Cover the pan with foil and bake until the eggplant is very tender when pierced with a fork, 40 to 45 minutes. Remove the pan and turn the oven to broil. Uncover the pan and place under the broiler to crisp up and char the tops of the kebab. Serve on or off the skewers, giving guests at least one skewer. Leftovers keep, refrigerated, for up to 5 days, and make for great lavash wraps when reheated.

Grape Leaf Tolma

Թ փո ղ   տո լ մա

stuffed grape leaves (vegetarian)

Tolma (or *dolma*, depending on who's doing the translation) is one of those foods that is universally loved in Armenia and in the diaspora. Lunchtime, a casual eatery in Yerevan, does brisk business in this version—a meatless one made with rice and seasonings—as well as several others. In Southern California, Ara's family has also made its share. And the truth is . . . they're not *that* different from one another. The key in this version is the mild tomatoey base and the addition of lemon juice to draw out flavor, which is important any time you serve something cold.

The best grape leaves unravel easily from the jar or can. American grape leaves can sometimes be too large or tough for tolma, so look for brands imported from Armenia, such as Avshar Prod (the label says "tinned grape leaves"), or other imported brands, such as Divina. Grape leaf tolma are best made a day or two before serving. Before you start, give yourself ample time for rolling and cooking tolma. Have a heavy-bottomed pot about 4 qt [4 L] in capacity, as well as a plate or pot lid that can lie inside the pot to help keep the tolma submerged as they cook. You can use any mild canned or home-made tomato sauce for this recipe. To dress the tolma up when serving, add a few thin slices of lemon to the plate.

-continued

Makes about 36 tolma

½ cup [120 ml] sunflower oil or other neutral oil

2 yellow onions, finely diced

½ cup [120 ml] tomato sauce

1 Tbsp tomato paste

1½ tsp kosher salt

1 tsp sweet paprika

½ tsp ground black pepper

½ tsp dried mint

½ cup [120 ml] lemon juice

1 heaping cup [225 g] long-grain white rice

One 15 to 16 oz [420 to 455 g] jar grape leaves (you may have extra)

In a soup pot over medium heat, warm ¼ cup [60 ml] of the oil. Add the onions and cook, stirring frequently, until they turn a medium-brown color, about 15 minutes, lowering the heat as necessary to prevent the onions from burning.

Pour in the remaining ¼ cup [60 ml] of oil. Stir in the tomato sauce, tomato paste, salt, paprika, pepper, mint, and ¼ cup [60 ml] of the lemon juice and cook for 3 more minutes, stirring occasionally. Add the rice, stir, and cook uncovered, stirring constantly to prevent the rice from scorching, until the rice swells up but is still a bit raw in the center, about 10 minutes. Remove the rice from the heat and set it aside to cool completely.

Rinse about 50 grape leaves under cold water. If there are still stems on the leaves, cut them off with scissors. Use the torn or damaged leaves to line the bottom and sides of a 4 qt [4 L] or

similar-size heavy-bottomed pot. Let some of the larger leaves hang over the sides of the pot.

On a clean counter, flatten out a leaf and place it vein-side up with the stem end closest to you. On the base of the leaf near the stem end, spoon about 1 heaping Tbsp of the rice filling into a log shape, keeping a border of about 1 in [2.5 cm] on the sides of the leaf. Fold the bottom left and bottom right edges of the leaf over the rice and then fold the sides over and roll it up snugly but not too tight, like a mini burrito. Place the roll seam-side down in the lined pot and repeat with the remaining leaves and filling. Once the bottom layer is full, stack the next layer with the rolls pointing in the opposite direction.

When all the rolls are in the pot, fold the extra leaves lining the sides of the pot over the top and drizzle in 1 cup [240 ml] of water and the remaining ¼ cup [60 ml] lemon juice.

Put a plate that fits inside of the pot on top of the rolls. Cover the pot with a lid and place on the stove. Bring the pot to a simmer, then decrease the heat as low as it will go and cook for 1 hour, or until all the water has evaporated. Take the pot off the heat and let the rolls cool down in the pot to room temperature.

Carefully remove the rolls from the pot and refrigerate for at least 2 hours or until completely cold. Cooked tolma keep, refrigerated, for up to 5 days.

Pasuts Tolma

Պասուց տոլմա

vegetarian cabbage rolls for Lent

"All Armenian women can cook," says Ruzanna Hovhannisyan, who happens to be a physicist. In her Yerevan flat, she served us a platter of these cabbage-wrapped bundles filled with chickpeas, lentils, and beans, a classic meat-free preparation made during Lent. (*Pas* means "for Lent.") With bulgur as a backdrop, the end result is rich in texture and protein, making it a perfect option to have on the table for a meatless meal.

-continued

Serves 4 to 6

Some women make *pasuts tolma* with fermented cabbage leaves, but you don't have to start with fermented leaves. For a tangy finish, we drizzle the tolma with vinegar before serving. In this method, we prepare the leaves by boiling the whole head of cabbage in water and then separating the leaves, which can be done a day ahead. If you'd rather cook dried beans and chickpeas for this recipe instead of using canned, read over Cooking Dried Beans (page 32) and use the bean cooking water to cook the tolma. Before you start, have a heavy-bottomed pot, about 4 to 6 qt [4 to 5.7 L] in capacity, and a stock pot ready.

CABBAGE LEAVES

2 Tbsp kosher salt

1 large head green cabbage

FILLING

2 Tbsp sunflower oil or other neutral oil

1 yellow onion, finely diced

One 15.5 oz [440 g] can chickpeas, drained

One 14 oz [400 g] can green or brown lentils, drained

One 15.5 oz [440 g] can red kidney beans, drained

1 cup [170 g] medium-grain bulgur

1 tsp sweet paprika

1 Tbsp tomato paste

2 tsp kosher salt

½ tsp ground black pepper

¼ cup [10 g] finely chopped cilantro

¼ cup [10 g] finely chopped flat-leaf parsley

1 Tbsp sliced opal basil (optional)

TO SERVE

1 Tbsp tomato paste

Juice of ½ lemon

3 Tbsp vinegar, for drizzling

To prepare the cabbage leaves, find a large pot that will fit the whole head of cabbage (at least 8 qt [7.5 L]). Fill the pot halfway with water, season with the salt, and bring to a boil.

With a sharp paring knife, cut out the core of the cabbage, but make sure the head stays intact. Have a large bowl of ice water and a towel-lined half-sheet pan ready. With a pair of tongs, carefully lower the cabbage into the water, cover the pot, and boil the cabbage on one side until the outer leaves begin to separate, about 4 minutes. Turn the heat off, pull off any of the outer cooked leaves, and plunge them into the ice water (they peel away easily when cooked). Rotate the cabbage to cook the other side, cover the pot, and bring it back to a boil. Cook the cabbage for 4 minutes. Turn the heat off, pull off more of the cooked cabbage leaves, and plunge them in the ice water. If any of the inner leaves look raw or refuse to pull apart without tearing, leave them in the water for another minute or two, then try to pull them off again. When all of the leaves have been cooked and chilled, drain the leaves and lay them out on the towel-lined pan.

To make the filling, heat the oil in a sauté pan over medium-high heat. Add the onion and cook, stirring often, until the onion softens and starts to brown on the edges, about 5 minutes. Transfer to a plate and let cool.

In a large mixing bowl, combine the chickpeas, lentils, kidney beans, bulgur, paprika, tomato paste, and cooled onions. Season with the salt, pepper, and herbs and mix thoroughly. You will have about 8 cups [2 L] of filling.

Line the bottom and sides of a 4 to 6 qt [4 to 5.7 L] heavy-bottomed pot or Dutch oven with the torn or damaged leaves. Leave some overhanging leaves on the side of the pot.

To roll the cabbage leaves, on a clean counter, working with one leaf at a time, flatten out a leaf and place it with the inside facing up and the stem end closest to you. On the base of the leaf near the stem, place ⅓ to ½ cup [85 to 115 g] of the filling, keeping a border of at least 1 in [2.5 cm] from the edge of the leaf. (If the cabbage leaf is a little smaller, use less filling so it's still easy to roll the leaf up.) Fold the left and right sides of the leaf over the filling and then roll it up tightly, starting from the bottom, like a burrito. Place the roll seam-side down in the lined pot. Continue filling and rolling until all of the filling is used. As you work, line up the tolmas nice and snug in the pot in one layer if possible. You will have about 16 rolls of various sizes.

To cook, mix the tomato paste with the lemon juice and pour it over the top. Fold the extra leaves lining the sides of the pot over the top and fill the pot with water until it reaches the top of the tolma. Cover the pot with a lid and place it on the stove. Bring the pot to a simmer, then decrease the heat to low and cook the tolma for 12 minutes, just enough time for the flavors to come together and the bulgur to hydrate.

Remove the pot from the heat and let it cool down for a few minutes. Pour off the extra water from the pot. Carefully lift the tolma out of the pot and transfer to a warmed serving platter. Drizzle the vinegar over the top. Leftover tolma keep, refrigerated, for up to 5 days.

Summer Tolma

Ամառային տոլմա

vegetables stuffed with meat and rice

Ruzanna Hovhannisyan, who shared her Pasuts Tolma recipe (page 174) with us, also made us a heap of summer tolma. So named because summer produce is hollowed out and then filled with a rice-and-meat stuffing, summer tolma is a colorful main course. Ruzanna started with the tomatoes first, using the insides to make a light tomato sauce. She then proceeded to hollow out the rest of the vegetables.

Serves 6

Ruzanna insists that summer tolma has to include at least three kinds of vegetables. The easiest to fill are stout bell peppers, followed by zucchini and then eggplant. The recipe makes about 6 cups [1.4 L] of filling. To give you a sense of how many vegetables you will need, bell peppers hold about ¾ cup [180 g] of filling, while hollowed-out zucchini and eggplant hold between ½ cup and 1 cup [120 and 240 g]. For eggplant, look for slender Italian or Japanese varieties and avoid round globe eggplant. Hollow them out with an apple corer or a metal vegetable peeler with a pointy top; you may also need to use a spoon to scrape out more of the filling. If there is extra filling and you have a few large tomatoes, cut the tops off the tomatoes, scoop out the tomato pulp, and add it to the pan. Stuff the insides with the filling, then cover the tomatoes with their tops and bake with the rest of the vegetables. If you make your own tomato sauce, feel free to use it in this recipe, though any mild canned tomato sauce works as well.

FILLING

1 cup [200 g] long-grain rice

1 lb [455 g] ground beef

½ lb [230 g] ground pork

½ yellow onion, finely diced

1 Anaheim pepper, cored, seeded, and finely chopped

½ cup [20 g] chopped flat-leaf parsley

¼ cup [10 g] chopped cilantro

2 Tbsp chopped dill

1 Tbsp sweet paprika

1 Tbsp kosher salt, plus more for seasoning

½ tsp dried thyme or dried summer savory

½ tsp ground black pepper

VEGETABLES

4 bell peppers of any color

2 smallish slender eggplants, preferably Italian (but not globe)

3 small zucchini

1 Tbsp kosher salt

COOKING

1¾ cups [420 ml] tomato sauce

½ cup [120 ml] water

1 Tbsp sunflower oil or other neutral oil

Preheat the oven to 400°F [200°C]. Lightly coat a rimmed 9 by 13 in [23 by 33 cm] or larger casserole pan with oil.

To make the filling, in a medium saucepan, cover the rice with 3 cups [720 ml] of water. Bring to a boil, lower to a simmer, and cook, uncovered, stirring occasionally, for 10 minutes. Drain the rice in a fine-mesh strainer and let cool to room temperature. It may still be slightly raw in the center, and that's okay.

Once the rice is cool, in a large bowl, mix together the rice, beef, pork, onion, Anaheim pepper, parsley, cilantro, dill, paprika, 1 Tbsp of salt, the thyme, and black pepper.

To prepare the vegetables, cut the tops off the bell peppers, reserving the tops. Shake out the seeds and pull out and discard any membranes.

-continued

With a vegetable peeler, peel strips away from the eggplants to give the sides a striped appearance. Trim the tops off and discard, then cut the eggplants in half crosswise into pieces roughly 5 in [12 cm] long. Using an apple corer or the tip of a swivel-head peeler, tunnel into the eggplants until nearly to the end, twist the corer, and then pull it out to remove the inner eggplant pulp. If the pulp is stubborn, use the tip of a small spoon to remove the insides. Hollow out the eggplants until their walls are about ¼ in [6 mm] thick. Cut the top off the zucchini. If they are long zucchini, cut them in half. Hollow out the zucchini with the corer as done for the eggplant, leaving one end closed. Finely chop the insides of the eggplant and zucchini and place in the prepared pan.

To fill the vegetables, season the hollowed-out vegetables evenly with salt both inside and outside. Using your hands, squish the filling into the vegetables, using as much as will fit. Cover the peppers with their tops.

Place the filled vegetables on top of the chopped eggplant and zucchini. Prop up the peppers, unless they are too narrow to be propped up. In that case, lay them on their sides. Lay the eggplant and zucchini on their sides. The vegetables can overlap—and they don't need to look perfect.

To cook, pour the tomato sauce and water over the top and drizzle with the oil. Bake until the vegetables are soft and the filling is cooked through and hot, 50 minutes to 1 hour. If the vegetables start to brown too fast, cover the pan with aluminum foil and continue to cook.

Let the vegetables rest for 10 minutes before gently transferring to a serving platter. Serve hot. Leftovers keep, refrigerated, for up to 5 days.

Braised Trout

Խաշած իշխան

Cherkezi Dzor, a restaurant in Gyumri, doubles as a hatchery. Put in an order and they kill the trout or sturgeon, grilling, poaching, or marinating the fish in myriad ways. (Their trout and sturgeon roe is also exceptional.) The property evolved from a place that sold live fish to a restaurant to eventually a hatchery, and today it's a fresh-fish institution in northern Armenia.

The Armenian term for this dish is "boiled trout," though we interpret it to be more of a braised preparation. The key with super-simple preparations like this one is ensuring that you start with good-quality, fresh trout. Serve it with a side of roasted or boiled potatoes seasoned with chopped parsley, Green Salad with Radishes (page 98), and a side of Matnakash (page 68).

-continued

Serves 4

2 whole trout (up to 2 lb [910 g] total) cleaned and scaled

1 Tbsp kosher salt

¼ yellow onion, sliced

4 allspice berries

2 bay leaves

½ tsp ground black pepper

Handful of flat-leaf parsley sprigs

½ cup [120 ml] water

Lemon wedges, for serving

Season the trout all over with the salt and refrigerate for 1 hour.

In a large, heavy-bottomed pot or Dutch oven (large enough to fit two trout comfortably without overlapping much), combine the onion, allspice berries, bay leaves, pepper, and parsley. Lay the trout on top and pour in the water.

Cover the pot with a lid, place over medium-low heat, and gradually bring the water to a simmer. Allow the trout to gently braise for 25 to 30 minutes, checking doneness once or twice. (The fewer times you remove the lid to check the fish, the less the steam escapes.)

To serve, transfer the trout to a warmed rimmed platter and spoon the braising juices and onion over the top. Serve with lemon wedges on the side. Braised trout is best the day it is made.

Lavash-Wrapped Trout

Իշխան լավաշի մեջ

We learned how to make this recipe from Nara Davtian, who in turn learned how to make it from her mother-in-law. Think of this dish as the French en *papiotte* style, wrapped in parchment paper, but even better because instead of paper, we're using lavash. Other than the method of how the fish is cooked, what's notable is the use of tarragon as the main seasoning for the trout, which gently imparts its anise flavor. If tarragon is out of reach, cilantro makes a good alternative, with a very different flavor.

-continued

Serves 2 generously, 4 as part of a larger meal

This is an easy recipe to make for more people; just add more fish and lavash and increase the seasonings. If the fish are very large, you may want to cut them into thirds rather than halves. You can make this dish with bone-in trout, but be sure to warn family and friends that they'll be taking the bones out of their fish parcels. Serve it with a Green Salad with Radishes (page 98).

1 Tbsp sweet paprika

1½ tsp kosher salt

2 butterflied (nearly boneless) trout (about 1 lb [455 g] total)

4 sheets homemade Lavash (page 48) or 2 sheets purchased lavash

4 Tbsp [60 g] unsalted butter, plus more for spreading on lavash

8 tarragon springs

Lemon wedges, for serving

Preheat the oven to 400°F [200°C]. Line a half-sheet pan with parchment paper or lightly oil it.

In a small bowl, mix together the paprika and salt.

To prepare each trout, trim off the fins with scissors, then cut the trout crosswise in half. One half will have the head and the other half will have the tail. Rub the salt blend inside and outside of the pieces, using all of the blend.

Trim each piece of lavash into a rectangle about 12 in [35 cm] long and 10 in [25 cm] wide. For each portion, place 1 Tbsp of butter and 2 sprigs of tarragon into the fish cavity, removing any tough stems if there are any. Place each trout piece parallel to the base of the short side of the lavash. Fold the left and right

sides of the lavash over the trout, then roll it up as if you were making a burrito.

Place the lavash packets, seam-side down, on the prepared baking sheet and spread a little bit of butter on top. Bake until the lavash is browned and crisp, about 20 minutes. Serve immediately with lemon wedges. Lavash-wrapped trout is best the day it is made.

Ghapama

Ղափամա

Some of Armenia's medieval monasteries look as if they've been pulled out of fairy tales, making a rice-filled Cinderella pumpkin feel as if it fits right into the narrative. But most Armenians think of this dish as the subject of an earworm of a folk song with a chorus that goes like this: "Hey, jan, ghapama!" (Hey, dear, ghapama!) The entire theme of the song is to draw attention to a pumpkin so delicious that everyone in the village should come to see it. (The lyrics following "Hey, jan" go on to say "tasty, delicious-scented ghapama!") It could have been easy for the folk song to drift into obscurity, but it enjoyed renewed attention thanks to Harout Pamboukjian, a Yerevan-born Armenian-American pop singer, who has performed it to sold-out crowds for decades. We've found that it's hard to resist singing the chorus any time this showstopper of a dish is at the table.

Make ghapama in the fall when the largest variety of winter squashes arrive at the market. Small, round pumpkins, such as Cinderella pumpkins, are perfect for the recipe. To cut off the top, it is handy to have pumpkin-carving knives. There are a few ways to approach making ghapama: Push it toward the savory side with caramelized onions, which is what we've done here, or leave the onions out and make it sweet with cinnamon. Shake Havan-Garapetyan, the owner of Artbridge restaurant in Yerevan, uses onions but also mixes in a little quince jam or marmalade for a subtle sweetness. (If you've made the Apricot Murabba on page 226, you can use the syrup in place of honey.) Ghapama can be served at the end of a meal in place of dessert, though John found that its sweet-savory combination made a perfect side dish for American Thanksgiving.

-continued

Serves 8 to 10

1 small pumpkin, about 5 lb [2.3 kg] and roughly 10 in [25 cm] wide

1 Tbsp kosher salt, plus more for seasoning

2 Tbsp honey

1½ cups [300 g] long-grain rice

2¼ cups [540 ml] water

4 Tbsp [60 g] unsalted butter, cubed

1 yellow onion, finely diced

½ cup [80 g] dried apricots, halved

¼ cup [35 g] sour cherries

5 pitted prunes, quartered

¾ cup [90 g] walnuts, coarsely chopped

¾ cup [90 g] slivered almonds

2 Tbsp apple cider vinegar

Arrange the oven racks to fit the pumpkin standing upright and preheat the oven to 350°F [180°C]. Line a half-sheet pan with aluminum foil.

Carefully cut out a wide lid around the stem at the top of the pumpkin as if making a jack-o'-lantern, reserving it to top the pumpkin once filled. Scoop out all the seeds and discard them or dry them out and save for another use. Place the pumpkin on the prepared pan. Season the insides with 2 tsp of the salt, rubbing it into the sides, and then drizzle in 1 Tbsp of the honey.

In a medium saucepan, combine the rice with 2 cups [480 ml] of the water. Cover and bring to a boil, lower to a simmer, and cook for 10 minutes, or until the rice is almost

(but not quite) cooked through. Transfer the rice to a large heatproof mixing bowl. It's okay if not all the water has absorbed into the rice.

Give the rice-cooking pan a rinse and melt 2 Tbsp of the butter in it over medium heat. Stir in the onion and sauté until softened and slightly golden brown, about 6 minutes. Add the onions to the bowl with the rice and then stir in the remaining 1 Tbsp of honey, the remaining 1 tsp of salt, and the apricots, sour cherries, prunes, walnuts, and almonds. Stir in the vinegar and taste the mixture, adding a few more pinches of salt, if desired.

Spoon the rice mixture into the pumpkin and pour in the remaining ¼ cup [60 ml] of water. Dot the remaining 2 Tbsp of butter on top. Cover the pumpkin with its lid and bake until the insides are hot and a toothpick slides easily into the flesh of the pumpkin, 1½ to 2 hours, rotating the pan halfway through (use two hands and be careful the pumpkin doesn't fall over). Let sit for 20 minutes so the rice can reabsorb the liquid. (The pumpkin acts as insulation, so the rice will stay hot.)

To serve, carefully transfer to a large round platter. Remove the lid and cut the pumpkin into wedges so the ghapama falls open like a sunflower, with the rice in the center. Serve salt at the table for extra seasoning. Leftovers keep, refrigerated, for up to 1 week. To make reheating the dish easier, store cut portions of pumpkin separately from the rice filling.

Lavash-Wrapped Etchmiadzin Kufta

Էջմիածնի էյուքթա լավաշի մեջ

Not often seen outside of Armenia, this recipe represents an old preparation in which cooks tenderized meat by pounding it between two stones while adding copious amounts of salt. It's not solely made in the city of Etchmiadzin (which is also the headquarters of the Armenian Apostolic Church), but that's where it's best known. The most common way to prepare this style of *kufta* is to shape the smooth meat into a ball, boil it, and serve it sliced with butter. Wrapping it in lavash—which is how Nara Davtian prepared it for us in Yerevan—elevates the texture, making it an unforgettable style of meatball encased in crispy bread.

-continued

Serves 6

In Armenia, the Etchmiadzin kufta meat comes mixed and seasoned at the butcher. Because we can't buy the same seasoned meat at American butcher shops, we re-created the recipe by using a food processor to prepare the meat. Read the blending method through before starting, and ensure that the meat is cold before blending. You can shape the lavash in two ways: either tied in a parcel (as shown on the facing page) or rolled up like a burrito, as is done for the Lavash-Wrapped Trout (page 183).

MEAT FILLING

1 lb [455 g] eye of round, cut into 1 in [2.5 cm] cubes and chilled

1 Tbsp kosher salt

1 cup [240 ml] cold water

¼ yellow onion, diced

1 garlic clove, coarsely chopped

1 large egg

2 Tbsp all-purpose flour

1 Tbsp vodka

1 tsp dried basil (preferably opal basil if available)

LAVASH WRAPS

6 sheets homemade Lavash (page 48) or 3 sheets purchased lavash

6 Tbsp [85 g] unsalted butter, at room temperature, plus more for spreading

6 sturdy chives or the green parts of green onions (for Parcel Method)

To make the meat filling, place the meat and the salt in a food processor and blend on high speed. After a minute or so, while the machine is running, drizzle in the water. Continue to blend, stopping once or twice to scrape down the sides of the processor, until the meat turns into a smooth, light-pink paste, about 6 minutes total. Transfer to a chilled mixing bowl.

In the same food processor (no need to wash it first), pulse together the onion and garlic until finely minced. Add the egg and continue to blend until nearly smooth. Return the meat to the food processor, sprinkle the flour on top, and process just until smooth. Return the filling to the mixing bowl.

Pour the vodka over the filling and sprinkle the basil on top. Using clean hands or a rubber spatula, stir the filling to incorporate the vodka while also mixing in air so the filling is light, not dense. It will look light pink to gray, and that's perfectly fine.

Preheat the oven to 350°F [180°C]. Line a half-sheet pan with parchment paper or lightly oil it. Pick one of the following options for shaping the lavash packets.

PARCEL METHOD Cut the lavash into six 10 inch [25 cm] square sheets. Keep the squares in a plastic bag so they don't dry out.

Place ⅓ cup [80 g] of the filling in the center of one square of lavash. Place 1 Tbsp of butter in the center of the mixture. Pull up all four corners

-continued

of the lavash and with 1 chive used in place of twine, tie a knot just above the filling to create a little parcel.

Place the parcel on the prepared pan, and repeat with the remaining lavash. Bake for 20 minutes, or until the tops are toasted golden brown and the insides are hot. (You can test this by putting the tip of a sharp knife into the center of each portion, and then touching the tip to see if it feels hot.)

BURRITO METHOD Cut the lavash into 6 strips about 7 in [17 cm] wide by 15 in [38 cm] long. Keep the cut lavash in a plastic bag so the strips don't dry out.

Position a strip of lavash with the short side closest to you. Place ⅓ cup [80 ml] of the filling along the base of the lavash, leaving the edges free. Add 1 Tbsp of butter into the center of the filling. Fold the left and right sides of the lavash over the filling, then roll it up as if you were making a burrito.

Place on the prepared pan seam-side down and repeat with the remaining lavash. Spread a little butter on the top of each portion and bake for 20 minutes, or until the tops are toasted golden brown and the insides are hot. (You can test this by putting the tip of a sharp knife into the center of each portion, and then touching the metal to see if it feels hot.)

Leftover kufta keeps, refrigerated, for about 3 days. Reheat in the oven until hot in the center.

Khashil

խաշիլ

savory toasted wheat porridge

A savory porridge made of toasted, crushed wheat berries served with yogurt and caramelized onions, *khashil* is for people who like hot cereal served on the savory side—though it's not thought of as a breakfast dish. In Askeran, a town in Artsakh that sits just past the ruins of an eighteenth-century fortress, Alla Hayrapetyan prepared khashil when making lunch for us at her family's restaurant. For presentation, Alla poured the cooked grains in a large bowl, spooning the onions in the center and making a moat of yogurt around the edges.

What elevates khashil from a forgettable porridge is toasting the wheat berries before grinding and cooking them, which gives them a stove-popped popcorn aroma. Toasting the wheat berries also makes it easier on the blades of a food processor or blender when crushing them. As far as which wheat berry to choose, white Sonora wheat berries are softer and grind up easier, but red wheat berries also work and grind in a flash in a high-powered blender. In a pinch, the old-fashioned American hot cereal Wheatena comes close to the toasted wheat flavor found in khashil.

-continued

Serves 4 as part of a larger meal

1 cup [190 g] wheat berries

4 cups [960 ml] water, plus more as needed

1 tsp kosher salt

1 Tbsp sunflower oil or other neutral oil

2 yellow onions, finely diced

About 1 cup [240 g] plain, whole-milk yogurt

In a dry sauté pan, heat the wheat berries over medium heat, stirring often, until the berries start to brown and smell aromatic, a little like popcorn kernels. Pulse the wheat berries in a high-powered blender or food processor until most of the grains are at least crushed a little but before it all turns to dust (there will be a mix of textures).

In a soup pot, bring the wheat berries, water, and salt to a boil. Stir well, decrease the heat to medium-low, cover, and cook for 30 minutes, stirring occasionally, until the wheat berries have cooked through and have absorbed most of the water. Turn off the heat, keep the pot covered, and let it sit for 20 minutes to allow the wheat berries to continue absorbing water.

Meanwhile, heat the oil in a sauté pan over medium heat. Add the onions and cook, stirring often, for 5 minutes, or until they begin to soften. Decrease the heat to low and continue to cook, stirring often, until the onions are very soft and golden brown, about 10 minutes more. If the bottom of the pan starts to burn at any point,

add 1 Tbsp of water and continue to cook, scraping the burned bits from the base of the pan with a wooden spoon.

To serve, spoon the wheat berries into a large serving bowl. Make a well in the center and add the onions. Drizzle the yogurt around the perimeter of the bowl to make a moat. Serve hot. Leftovers keep, refrigerated, for up to 5 days. Reheat by gently simmering the porridge on the stove with a splash of water.

Harissa

Հարիսա

wheat berry porridge with chicken

This is one of the most deceptively understated dishes in Armenia, and one of the oldest—and it has nothing to do with the condiment from North Africa with the same name. Instead, *harissa* comes from the word *havel*, "to whisk or beat." It's a simple, savory porridge cooked so that the grains are creamy and the meat is so soft as to be barely visible. This classic dish serves as a historical link between Eastern and Western Armenians. In the village of Musaler near Zvartnots Airport, pots and pots of harissa are served on the third Sunday of September to commemorate the 1915 siege of Musa Dagh (*Musa Ler* in Armenian). During the genocide, Armenian villagers cornered at this mountainside along the Mediterranean coastline fought off Ottoman soldiers for fifty-three days until they were rescued by French and British warships. All they had to eat at this time was harissa.

In modern Armenia, harissa is also an ordinary family food. Because everyone gets the same amount of grains and meat, it is the ultimate democratic way to serve a crowd. Today, chicken is the most common protein, and getting a good-quality bird goes a long way to ensuring good flavor, because it also flavors the broth. The traditional way relayed to us by Yerevan local Tatev Malkhasyan is to simmer a chicken cut into pieces in water for several minutes before adding more than 2 lb [1 kg] of wheat berries.

Serves 4 to 6

This recipe uses only 2 chicken legs, though with a reduced amount of grains for a slightly meatier outcome. To achieve the signature creamy porridge texture, stir the grains and the meat together thoroughly at the end. Harissa is the ultimate stick-to-your ribs meal. It's designed to stand alone, though, like most meals in Armenia, there's bound to be an herb and cheese plate (see page 35), lavash, pickles, and fresh tomatoes and cucumbers on the table as well.

2 whole chicken legs (thigh and drumstick attached)

8 cups [2 L] water

2 tsp kosher salt, plus more for seasoning

2 cups [360 g] pearled farro (see Note)

Unsalted or salted butter, for serving

Pull the chicken skins off the legs and place the legs in a 6 qt [5.7 L] heavy-bottomed pot or Dutch oven. Pour in the water and add the salt. Bring the pot to a boil, then lower to a gentle simmer and cook for 20 minutes to flavor the water, skimming away any scum from the surface.

Ladle out 2 cups [480 ml] of the cooking water and reserve. Stir the farro into the pot and bring to a boil. Turn the heat to low, stir the pot again, then cover and cook for 40 minutes, checking once or twice that the grains aren't scorching and turning the chicken pieces over occasionally.

Remove the lid and transfer the chicken to a bowl. The meat will have started to pull away from the bone and will be tender. Cover the pot so the grains can continue to absorb the broth.

After 15 minutes or whenever the chicken is cool enough to handle, remove the bones and shred the chicken into small pieces. Stir the chicken back into the pot with 1 cup [240 ml] of the reserved cooking water, bring to a boil, then lower the heat to medium and cook, stirring constantly, for 3 to 5 minutes, or until the porridge starts to look creamy and the chicken pieces are blended well into the grains. If the porridge looks dry (or if you prefer a looser porridge), ladle in the remaining cooking water. Taste, seasoning with more salt, if desired.

To serve, spoon the harissa into bowls and top each serving with a pat of butter. Serve immediately. Leftovers keep, refrigerated, for up to 5 days. Reheat by gently simmering the porridge on the stove with a splash of water.

NOTE: While pearled farro is not the traditional form of grain in harissa, the results of this recipe are very close in flavor and texture to the harissa we sampled in Armenia. White Sonoran wheat berries are another option, though depending on the wheat berries themselves, they may take more water and cooking time. If using them, ensure the wheat berries are cooked through before mixing the porridge with the chicken.

Kurkut

Կուրկում

wheat berry porridge with duck

The Artsakh answer to Armenia's Harissa (page 196) is kurkut. The word itself means both the crushed wheat berries and a savory porridge made with either pork or duck. In Mets Tagher, a hillside village in Artsakh, we saw trays of wheat berries drying at a restaurant that had a stone mill to crush them for kurkut. (No matter where you are in this part of the world, wheat berries will find you.)

The biggest difference between kurkut and harissa is how the ingredients are cooked. Instead of being stirred together, they are layered and allowed to gently braise, explains Carmen Harutunyan, an Artsakh native who now lives in Yerevan. Because replicating the exact type of wheat berry is challenging in the United States, we use unpearled farro, which is a darker red than pearled farro. You can also make kurkut with hard red winter wheat berries, though they may require more time to cook. The best accompaniment for kurkut is a side of Salt-Brined Cucumber Pickles (page 133) to cut through the richness, as well as an herb and cheese plate (see page 35) and Tonir Hats (page 73). While not traditional, we also like serving a dish of sour cherries and onions alongside, to bring out the flavor of the duck.

-continued

Serves 6

6 whole duck legs (thigh and drumstick attached)

2 cups [360 g] farro (preferably unpearled) or hard red winter wheat berries

2 tsp kosher salt, plus more for seasoning

5 cups [1.2 L] water, plus more as needed

1 cup [165 g] dried sour cherries

2 Tbsp apple cider vinegar

2 Tbsp sunflower oil or other neutral oil

2 yellow onions, thinly sliced

Arrange the oven racks to be able to accommodate a 6 qt [5.7 L] or similar-size Dutch oven or heavy-bottomed saucepan and preheat to 300°F [150°C].

Pull the skins off the duck legs, using a paring knife to help detach the skin. (It's okay if some of the skin is left around the drumsticks.) With the knife, separate the thighs from the drumsticks. Place 1 cup [180 g] of the farro at the base of the Dutch oven and arrange the thighs and legs in one layer as much as possible. Season with half of the salt, then cover with the remaining 1 cup [180 g] farro and season with the remaining salt. Pour in the water, bring to a boil, then turn off the heat, cover, and transfer to the oven.

Bake for 1 hour, then check to see how much water has been absorbed by the farro. If the pot is looking dry, pour in 1 cup [240 ml] water. Cover and continue to cook for 1 hour more, or

until the farro is soft and the duck is very tender when pierced with a fork.

In a small bowl mix the cherries and vinegar together. Warm the oil in a sauté pan over medium-high heat. Add the onions, lower the heat to medium, and gently cook, stirring often, until the onions soften and start to look translucent but before they become completely soft and brown, about 4 minutes. Stir in the cherries and vinegar, season with a few pinches of salt, and cook briefly until the vinegar has reduced. Remove from the heat. (This can be made ahead of time and served at room temperature.)

Uncover the Dutch oven and place it on the stove over medium heat. (It is okay if the porridge look a little watery at this stage.) Bring to a simmer and cook, checking the bottom with a wooden spoon to ensure it's not burning, until the porridge reaches the desired consistency—some like it soupier while others prefer it to be as thick as oatmeal.

Divide the duck and farro among 6 bowls and serve with the onions and sour cherries on the side. Leftovers keep, refrigerated, for up to 5 days. Reheat by gently simmering the porridge on the stove with a splash of water.

Panrkhash

Պանրխաշ

lavash and cheese bake

You know when you taste something and you think there's no way so much flavor comes from so few ingredients? *Panrkhash* is one of those things. On his first trip to Armenia, John ate it in Gyumri and was baffled that a dish could be made simply with strips of lavash, some onion, some water, butter, and cheese. We knew we needed to find out more. At Old Armenia, a classic restaurant in Gyumri, we watched as chef Armenuhi Marukyan layered lavash pieces with shredded cheese, caramelized onion, and a generous amount of melted butter. Then she poured hot water over the top. The whole thing looked, well, dubious—until it was baked and a golden miracle of bread and cheese emerged from the oven. Could mac and cheese ever be this good?

-continued

Serves 4

If you're using store-bought lavash, look for classic Armenian-style lavash, the thinnest kind you can find. You will need approximately 2 sheets of purchased lavash. If using home-made Lavash (page 48), have at least 6 sheets just to be on the safe side, to avoid coming up short. For a stronger cheese flavor, crumble in a little blue cheese with the string cheese.

½ cup [115 g] plus 1 Tbsp [15 g] unsalted butter, plus more for buttering the bowls

6 sheets homemade Lavash (page 48) or 3 sheets purchased lavash

½ yellow onion, finely diced

2 cups [170 g] shredded and chopped string cheese

2 cups [480 ml] hot water

Preheat the oven to 450°F [230°C]. Butter two 6 in [15 cm] wide ovenproof bowls or ramekins.

Cut two 6 in [15 cm] squares of lavash (these will cover the top of each bowl). Cut the remaining lavash into 1 in [2.5 cm] squares.

In a saucepan over medium-high heat, melt ½ cup [115 g] of the butter. Add the onion and sweat until softened, about 4 minutes. Remove the pot from the heat.

To assemble the panrkhash, in each bowl, build up four layers, alternating ½ cup [21 g] lavash squares and ¼ cup [21 g] cheese and ending with cheese. Top each bowl with half of the onion-butter mixture and pour 1 cup [240 ml] of the hot water over the top of each bowl.

Place 1 lavash square over each bowl and dot each square with half of the remaining 1 Tbsp of butter.

Bake until the tops of the lavash squares are golden brown and the cheese is bubbling and melted, 10 to 15 minutes. Leftover panrkhash keeps, refrigerated, for up to 5 days. Reheat in a 350°F [180°C] oven until hot all the way through.

Chanakh

Չանախ

braised oxtail with vegetables, beans, and chickpeas

When we stopped by to meet students at the TUMO campus in Gyumri, we asked them what dishes summed up Gyumri food. The first answer was *kalla*, a braised cow's or lamb's head, which John had eaten on his last trip to Gyumri at the historic restaurant Poloz Mukuch. "What else?" we asked, knowing that kalla would be a little challenging to re-create at home. "*Chanakh!*" the class said, referencing a dish of braised oxtails, beans, lentils, and vegetables. Instead of a cow's head, we were going with a cow's tail.

Serves 4 or 5

In Armenia, chanakh can mean many things, from a salty cow's milk cheese to the earthenware pottery used for cooking stews. In this case, it also means a rich stew in which the oxtail and vegetables are added in layers. Inspired by the chanakh served at Old Armenia, a restaurant in Gyumri, this version is filled with a variety of beans and vegetables. When buying oxtails, look for pieces cut about 2 in [5 cm] thick. Because the tip of an oxtail is thinner than the top end, the pieces will range in width. If making this the day before you plan to serve it, cook the oxtails until tender and then refrigerate them. Before serving, use a spoon to scrape off any extra fat from the surface and then bring the chanakh to a simmer before adding the vegetables. You can opt to remove the bones before serving. A little spritz of lemon at the end highlights the richness of the braise.

3½ to 4 lb [1.6 to 1.8 kg] oxtail pieces (about 10 pieces in a mix of sizes)

5 tsp kosher salt

2 Tbsp sunflower oil or other neutral oil

1 yellow onion, diced

1 Tbsp all-purpose flour

3 Tbsp tomato paste

5 cups [1.2 L] water

1 bay leaf

1 Tbsp sweet paprika

½ tsp ground black pepper

2 Anaheim peppers, cored, seeded, and sliced into strips

1 large tomato, sliced

2 large Yukon gold potatoes, cubed

18 green beans or 10 pieces okra, halved

One 15.5 oz [440 g] can kidney beans, drained

One 15.5 oz [440 g] can chickpeas, drained

2 garlic cloves, minced

2 Tbsp chopped flat-leaf parsley

2 Tbsp chopped cilantro

2 Tbsp chopped opal basil (optional)

1 lemon, cut into wedges (optional)

If the oxtails have an outer layer of fat, trim it off but don't remove the membrane that surrounds the meat—this helps it stay attached to the bone. Season the oxtails with 2 tsp of the salt.

Have a large plate and a pair of tongs handy. Heat the oil in a 6 qt [5.7 L] heavy-bottomed pot or Dutch oven over medium-high heat. In 2 batches, add the oxtail pieces in a single layer and brown all sides, turning the pieces with tongs as they sear, for about 8 minutes per batch. If the bottom of the pot starts to burn, lower the heat. Transfer the seared pieces to the plate and repeat with the remaining meat, leaving any fat in the pot.

Turn the heat to medium, add the onion, and sweat until softened, about 4 minutes. Stir in the flour so that it coats the onion pieces, then stir in the tomato paste until thoroughly mixed in. Pour in 1 cup [240 ml] of the water, breaking up any clumps of tomato paste before adding the remaining 4 cups [1 L] water. Season with 2 tsp of the salt, the bay leaf, paprika, and black pepper.

-continued

Return the oxtails to the pot and bring the pot to a brisk simmer. Turn the heat to low, cover, and simmer for 2½ to 3 hours, or until the oxtails begin to feel tender when pierced with a fork. (Be patient; oxtail requires more time to become tender than other braising cuts of meat.) Check the pot periodically to ensure it maintains a lazy bubble but never boils.

Remove the lid and use a ladle to remove some of the fat on the surface. At this point, the meat can be cooled and refrigerated in its braising liquid. (If doing so, scoop off and discard the excess fat before reheating.) Bring the pot back to a simmer. Stir in the Anaheim peppers, tomato, and potatoes, and season with the remaining 1 tsp of salt. Simmer for 15 to 20 minutes, or until the potato is tender when pierced with a fork. Stir in the green beans and simmer until nearly cooked through, about 5 minutes more. Stir in the kidney beans, chickpeas, and garlic, bring back to a simmer, and cook until the beans are hot all the way through. The sauce should look thinner than a chowder but thicker than a braise. If it is too thick, add a splash of water to loosen it up. Let the chanakh rest for 20 minutes before serving to allow the meat to absorb some of the braising liquid.

To serve, divide the oxtail pieces among serving bowls, offering a mix of large and small pieces. Spoon the vegetables and sauce over the top and garnish with the chopped herbs. Serve with lemon wedges on the table. Leftover chanakh keeps for up to 5 days in the refrigerator or 1 month in the freezer.

Gyumri

The best beer in Armenia is Alexandrapol, which comes in a stout, amber bottle from the north-west city of Gyumri, the second largest city in the country. Taking its name from a period of time when the city was a culturally vibrant part of the Russian Empire in the nineteenth century, the mellow beer embraces throwback branding. More importantly, its existence is a sign that Gyumretsis are taking back their city from its tragic twentieth-century existence and reestablishing itself as a place for culture, arts, and good food and drink.

On December 7, 1988, a deadly earthquake hit the city—then called Leninakan—leveling buildings and killing thousands in the city and surrounding areas. Rebuilding efforts moved slowly in the months and years that followed until the Soviet Union collapsed. Then they virtually came to a halt as a newly independent Armenia grappled with fighting a war with Azerbaijan and handling countrywide food and fuel shortages. Even today, the city has a generation of elderly residents living in subpar housing, their lives forever affected by the earthquake's destruction.

The twenty-first century promises change, and signs of construction are everywhere. In the center of the city, carved details on doors and the facades of slate-gray buildings give the city a feeling of being part of another, grander

age, and there's a growing sense of optimism in Gyumri that these relics can help the city reclaim its nineteenth-century reputation as an important cultural hub in the Caucasus. On a rainy spring day in 2018, we dodged puddles and weaved through vendor booths as Marie Lou Papazian, the director of TUMO, took us on a tour of the downtown farmers' market, where she is working to restore the covered marketplace. She also walked us through the old, grand Soviet theater in Central Park, which was in the process of being rebuilt.

Gyumretsis, despite their history, are famous in Armenia for their sense of humor. Born in the late nineteenth century, Mkrtich Melkonyan was the city's most famous humorist, known for telling jokes, especially after a few pints. Better known as Poloz Mukuch (poloz—a colloquial term meaning "out of proportion"—being a jab at Melkonyan's lanky stature), his legacy lives on at an eponymous beerhouse of the same name in a building that dates back to the Alexandrapol era. The historical landmark also serves hearty fare, from khashlama, a beef or lamb stew, to Gyumri's signature dish, kalla. Walk out the door from Poloz Mukuch and you'll be facing the Gyumri Brewery, which just so happens to make Alexandrapol beer. The city has a ways to go in its rebuilding efforts, but it's already proven to be a place to eat and drink well.

Khashlama

խաշլամա

beef or lamb stew

Made with beef or lamb, *khashlama* translates to "boiled meat," though "stew" is a more accurate description. Essentially, it's unpretentious comfort food that takes advantage of good-quality meat. Some cooks keep it austere by only adding salt and potatoes; others make it more festive with peppers and tomatoes. This version takes khashlama in the latter direction, giving it a bountiful—if still humble—appearance.

Cooking the potatoes in a separate pot ensures they cook evenly and makes it easier to reheat the stew without the potatoes falling apart. But if you'd rather cook the potatoes in the same pot, add them 20 minutes before the stew is done cooking; they'll finish cooking and absorb flavor as they rest in the cooking liquid for 15 minutes after removing the stew from the heat. While it isn't typical, a little Aleppo pepper sprinkled on top perks up the flavors.

Serves 4 to 6

STEW

2½ lb [1.2 kg] lamb or beef stew meat, trimmed of sinew and cut into 1 to 2 in [2.5 to 5 cm] cubes

1 Tbsp kosher salt, plus more for seasoning

½ tsp ground black pepper

1 Tbsp sunflower oil or other neutral oil

4 cups [960 ml] water

2 yellow onions, cut into wedges

1 bay leaf

4 Roma tomatoes, quartered lengthwise

2 Anaheim peppers, cored, seeded, and quartered

TO FINISH

4 Yukon gold potatoes, peeled and quartered

Kosher salt

¼ cup [10 g] chopped flat-leaf parsley

¼ cup [10 g] chopped dill

Crushed dried red pepper (optional)

To make the stew, season the meat evenly with the salt and pepper.

Heat the oil in a 6 qt [5.7 L] heavy-bottomed pot or Dutch oven over medium-high heat. Scatter the meat in as even a layer as possible and let cook, undisturbed, for 10 minutes, or until the meat begins to brown on one side.

Pour in the water, then stir in the onions and bay leaf. (It's okay if some of the onion sticks out of the water.) Bring to a boil, then lower to a very gentle simmer, cover, and cook for 50 minutes, stirring once or twice and checking to ensure the liquid isn't boiling (which may make the meat tough).

Stir in the tomatoes and Anaheim peppers, and cook, uncovered, until the meat is tender when pierced with a fork, about 30 minutes more. Let the meat rest in the braising liquid for at least 15 minutes before serving.

Place the potatoes and a few pinches of salt in a large pot and cover with water. Bring to a boil, lower to a simmer, and cook until the potatoes are tender when pierced with a fork, about 15 minutes. If the potatoes are nearly there but need a little more time, turn off the heat and let them sit in the hot water for 5 minutes more. Drain.

To serve, bring the khashlama back to a simmer and have a warmed rimmed platter ready. Place the potatoes on the platter and spoon the khashlama on top and around the potatoes, adding the braising liquid on top. Sprinkle the parsley, dill, and red pepper, if using, over the top. Leftovers keep, refrigerated, for up to 5 days or frozen for up to 2 months. To reheat, gently bring the stew to a simmer on the stove.

Tjvjik

Sdվդիկ

sautéed liver, offal, and onions

Forget all of the consonants in tjvjik and think instead of the sound of a knife hitting a cutting board: *tij, vij, jik*. This dish of chopped liver, onions, and offal meat is so beloved in Armenia that it became the premise of a short film named after the dish. In the film, a rich man catches a penniless man staring at a plump liver at the butcher shop. Amused by the desperate look on the poor man's face, the rich man buys him the liver and implores him to enjoy a nice meal of tjvjik.

Though the poor man never gets his tjvjik meal, that scene sets the stage for understanding the passion behind this dish of finely chopped innards and onions. Our most memorable tjvjik experience came in the back of a butcher shop in Yerevan run by Samvel Hayrapetyan. Samvel went to work slicing lamb liver, kidneys, heart, and lungs against a cutting board formed from the stump of a tree. He then gently cooked the pieces, letting lamb tail fat render into the pan before adding the liver so it didn't overcook. To serve it, he wrapped a mound of tjvjik and raw onions in lavash for each of us and doled out shots of vodka with Coke chasers. "There might be people who make it better than I do, but what's most important is the feeling you give people when they eat it," he said. "*Kenats!*" we cheered.

We've adapted this recipe to make use of offal meats that are more accessible in the United States. If lamb offal is hard to find, you can use beef liver.

Serves 4

1 lb [455 g] lamb hearts, cut into 1 in [2.5 cm] cubes (about 2 hearts)

8 oz [230 g] lamb kidneys, cut into 1 in [2.5 cm] cubes (about 2 kidneys)

1 lb [455 g] lamb liver, cut into 1 in [2.5 cm] cubes

3 Tbsp unsalted butter

12 oz [340 g] rib eye, cut into 1 in [2.5 cm] cubes

1 yellow onion, thinly sliced

1 tsp sweet paprika

1 tsp kosher salt

½ tsp ground black pepper

1 Tbsp chopped cilantro

1 Tbsp chopped flat-leaf parsley

1 Tbsp chopped opal basil (optional)

1 tsp chopped dill

TO SERVE

4 sheets homemade Lavash (page 48) or 2 sheets store-bought lavash

¼ yellow onion, thinly sliced

Lemon wedges

Rinse the hearts, kidneys, and liver pieces in cold water and drain. Set the liver aside.

Select a large sauté pan or saucepan that has a lid. In the pan, melt the butter over medium-high heat. Add the hearts, kidneys, and rib eye, cover the pan, and decrease the heat to medium-low. Simmer gently, stirring occasionally, for 25 to 30 minutes, or until the hearts and kidneys start to feel tender when pierced with a fork. A good amount of liquid will accumulate in the pan, which will eventually become the sauce.

Stir in the onion, paprika, salt, and pepper, cover the pan again, and gently simmer for 15 minutes more.

Stir in the liver, cover the pan again, and gently simmer for 10 to 15 more minutes, checking the liver often to ensure it remains slightly pink inside (avoid overcooking it or it will become grainy). Stir in the herbs and taste, seasoning with more salt, if desired.

Serve hot, offering lavash and onions for guests to make their own wraps and lemon wedges if they want a squeeze of lemon on top. Tjvjik is best the day it's made but leftovers can be kept, refrigerated, for up to 3 days. To reheat, gently bring the tjvjik to a simmer with a splash of water.

Ancient Wine in the Twenty-First Century

In an industrial district of Yerevan, Vahe Keushguerian and his daughter, Aimee, greeted us at the door of a warehouse and led us to an experiment. A small batch of Kaputkeni grapes were fermenting with their skins, and the mash of purple-blue in the vat resembled a blueberry smoothie. Vahe siphoned off some of the juice for us to taste, and just like that, we realized that we had officially entered Armenia's winemaking frontierland, a place where experimenting with this blue-hued grape—and countless other varieties that were brushed aside in favor of grapes that were easier to grow—is not only normal but necessary if Armenia is to reclaim its heritage as a destination for wine. This warehouse, WineWorks, is Vahe's winery incubator, and it's playing a big part in the growing movement to define Armenia's place in the world of wine.

Armenia is both one of the youngest and oldest winemaking areas in the world. It's likely the Vitis vinifera vines—the grape species used in fine wine—originated in the Caucasus. While older traces of wine have been found in Georgia and Iran, the world's oldest known winery was dug up only a few hours from Yerevan. Visible from the highway that runs through the province of Vayots Dzor, the Areni-1 archaeological cave complex dates back 6,100 years. Areni is also the name of Armenia's signature red grape, which makes a medium-bodied wine that brings to mind sour cherries, dried herbs, and spices. Here, the Arpa River, which runs alongside the town, helps regulate weather extremes while the volcanic soil yields mineral-rich fruit.

Unlike Georgia, whose winemaking traditions were undisrupted for centuries, Armenia's vineyards have been subjected to the whims of other interests. In the nineteenth century, Russian czars preferred using Armenia's grapes for brandy production, a tradition that continued under the Soviets. To meet the volume of grapes needed for brandy, yields were prized over flavor, and underperforming vines were destroyed or neglected. Later, more vines were pulled out in the 1980s as part of President Mikhail Gorbachev's anti-alcohol campaign.

It's only been in the past decade that winemaking in Armenia has taken off in earnest, though countless challenges remain. Vineyards in Armenia grow at high altitudes and often in extreme conditions. Domestically, wine is pricier than vodka, beer, or brandy. Abroad, the grape varieties are unfamiliar and hard to pronounce. Even the right equipment and supplies are hard to come by; to make Keush, a sparkling wine made in the traditional method used in Champagne, Aimee Keushguerian had to import the special bottles as well as all of the equipment.

Efforts also need to be made to reclaim winemaking heritage, starting with revitalizing local grapes. Voskehat is the most important white grape of the moment, making mineral-rich white wines that can carry floral aromas. Down the road from the Areni cave, Trinity Canyon Vineyards is experimenting with an orange wine made by macerating Voskehat grapes with their skins in terra-cotta karas, Armenian amphora. While these vessels are familiar among natural winemakers in Georgia and parts of Europe, they also were vital to Armenia's ancient winemaking traditions, and several have been found buried in the Areni

-continued

caves. Yet Armenia is still primarily known for its red wine, and not all of it from Areni. Growing in Artsakh's clay-rich soils, the red grape Sireni (also called Khndoghni) yields a more full-bodied wine, and one that winemakers hope will age well.

Despite the challenges, Armenian winemakers are enthusiastic about the future. There's a sense of camaraderie, of sharing ideas about how to manage extreme viticulture—the high altitudes, volcanic soil, remote roads, and bone-dry summers—and of propagating the best cuttings of local grapes. Could Kaputkeni become the next Areni? What's clear is that it's rare to taste new wines that come wrapped in one of the world's best origin stories.

A Summer's Thorn Is a Winter's Sweet

Fruit Preserves and Baked Treats

he exact proverb that inspired this chapter is "a summer's thorn is a winter's almond" (Ամառվա փուշը ձմերվա նուշն է), and it's based on the premise of doing things today to reap the benefits later. In a land known for long, cold winters, with limited—if any—access to an outside food supply, being able to preserve summer produce had strategic value. Even today, the practice of preserving fruit is going strong. Markets are filled with heaps of dried fruit, sheets of sour lavash (fruit leathers), and several ingenious fruit-and-nut preserves. In homes, pantries overflow with jars filled with kompot and jams, making a summer sweet accessible any time of the year.

The recipes in this chapter start with ways to preserve fruit, from the simple, such as Kompot (page 221), a sweet fruit drink with pieces of fruit at the bottom, to the more involved, like Sweet Soujuk (page 229), a preserve involving threading walnuts on a string, dipping them in thickened grape juice, and stringing the strands up to dry. The second half of the chapter focuses on classic baked or cooked treats that are perfect to serve alongside *soorj*, small cups of Armenian coffee, and *urtz*, Armenian thyme tea. You'll find our version of Gata (page 235), a classic Armenian pastry filled with walnuts; Halva (page 232), a buttery treat made of four ingredients and cooked on the stove; and a version of baklava (page 239) we learned how to make in the southern Armenian city of Goris.

All this to say that with some preparation, the unappreciated bounties of the summer—like a backyard tree dropping more fruit than you can eat, or a windfall of walnuts that you wonder when you'll have time to actually shell—can be savored in the winter or any other time of the year.

Hot Drinks

The everyday ritual of drinking coffee or tea is a social occasion in Armenia, usually accompanied with something sweet to offset the bitterness of the drink. It could be as simple as a foil-wrapped chocolate or a spoonful of *murabba*, a fruit preserve eaten straight, or more elaborate, like baklava.

COFFEE

Soorj is Armenian coffee, and it's neither espresso nor drip. Instead, it's what many in the United States think of as Middle Eastern coffee, a style in which finely ground beans are brewed on the stove and then served in small demitasse cups. It's also what fuels the country. Today, nearly every meeting or visit begins with soorj. At a bakery we visited in Gyumri, store manager Varduhi Grigoryan ran home to get enough china to serve us all a cup, even though the bakery was busy with orders. Yet the most unexpected soorj moment came from the time Ara took a cab to Mount Aragats, the highest point in Armenia.

> "Do you like *dak soorj*?" the driver asked him.

> "Sure—I like hot coffee."

The driver pulled over, took out a 100-dram coin, plopped it into a vending machine, and presented Ara with a thimble's worth of coffee. "Dak Soorj!" he exclaimed.

To make soorj at home, buy preground Armenian coffee (it may also be called "Arabic coffee"). Home coffee grinders do not grind beans fine enough, and the powdery grind is essential for allowing the coffee to dissolve into the water and form a nice froth on top. Spoon 1 heaping tsp of coffee per serving into a *jazzve* (a coffee pot for the stove) or small saucepan. Cover with 3 oz [90 ml] of water per serving and gradually bring to a boil. Foam will start to rise to the surface. At this point, turn the heat off, then bring it back to a boil briefly. Remove the pot from the heat and then spoon the froth into each demitasse before pouring in the coffee. Guests can ask for it with sugar (*kakhtsr*), or without (*tarrn*); for those who want sugar, just add a little to their demitasse before pouring in the coffee.

TEA

In Armenia, tea is just as often an herbal tisane as it is a caffeinated beverage. In addition to imported black and green teas, Herbs and Honey, a modern tea shop in Gyumri, provides a long list of local herbs to choose from, including wild mint, rose hips, dried opal basil, and chamomile, all of which come with a description of what they remedy, from alleviating stress to aiding digestion.

The most common way to experience tea in Armenia is to have *urtz*, a tea made of dried thyme and dried savory. It's also sometimes blended with dried mint for a lively but mellow green-yellow-hued tea that calms the nerves after so many demitasses of soorj. You can buy urtz in tea bags at tourist shops, but the most genuine way to buy it is in bulk to be brewed like loose-leaf tea. Add a large scoopful of the dried herbs to a teapot, pour just-boiled water (about 200°F [95°C]) over the top, and let it steep for 3 to 5 minutes, or until it turns a golden-green color (any longer and it could taste bitter). The first cup of urtz may taste unusually grassy, but the more you have it, the more soothing—and addictive—urtz becomes.

Kompot

Կոմպոտ

fruit drink with whole fruit pieces

A relic from Soviet times, kompot in Armenia is a drink made of mostly water, some sugar, and whole pieces of fruit—and it has nothing to do with the Western idea of compote, a bowl of cooked fruit. Created as another way to use up in-season fruit or preserve it for later, kompot is a refreshing drink any time of the year. At feasts, it plays a key role as a chaser for vodka.

-continued

Makes 1½ qt [1.4 L]

Kompot takes on the color of whatever fruit is used, turning pale orange with apricots and deep red with cherries. This recipe uses apricots, but you can also opt for any mix of cherries (pictured on facing page), berries, and stone fruit, making this the perfect thing to prepare when you're cleaning out the fridge. While this version is light on sweetness compared to some types of kompot, it can often be made quite sweet (and if you'd like it sweeter, simply up the sugar content). For the true kompot experience, be sure to eat the fruit pieces that settle at the bottom of the glass.

6 ripe apricots (about 1⅓ lb [600 g])

8 cups [2 L] water

½ cup [100 g] granulated sugar

Halve the apricots and remove the pits.

In a large pot, bring the water to a boil and add the sugar. Cook, stirring occasionally, until the sugar has dissolved. Add the apricots and simmer until the fruit is soft when pierced with a fork but still holds its shape, about 5 minutes. Pour the kompot into a heatproof pitcher or large jar and refrigerate. Serve cold or at room temperature. Kompot keeps, refrigerated, for up to 7 days.

Plum Sour Lavash

Թթու լավաշ

fruit leather

Essentially a different way to say fruit leather, sour lavash is made by drying pureed fruit in a thin sheet that you can tear and roll however you please—which is one of the reasons that kids (like Ara's son, Zach) like it so much. The best time of the year to make sour lavash is in the summer when stone fruits and other seasonal favorites are inexpensive. We chose plums for this rendition because the sour skins balance out the sweetness of the fruit and add color, but apricots, cherries, and grapes also yield terrific sour lavash.

Makes one 13 by 18 in [23 by 33 cm] sheet

In Armenia, the puree dries in the sun, but we modified the recipe to use a low oven, letting the sour lavash dry out overnight. The ideal temperature is around 150°F [65°C], but a lot of ovens only go as low as 170°F [75°C]. You can still make sour lavash at 170°F [75°C], with a few adjustments: If you notice the edges are becoming dry and hard but the center is still sticky, try wedging the oven door open a crack to let extra moisture out as it dries. Alternatively, if you have a gas oven, try leaving the lavash in the oven overnight to let it dry solely by the power of the pilot light. The time it takes to dry the lavash varies anywhere between 9 and 14 hours, depending on the fruit, the humidity in the air, and the temperature used for drying. You know it's ready when it peels easily off the parchment paper or Silpat (a reusable nonstick liner for sheet pans). Every once in a while, a batch sticks to the parchment paper, which might mean that the parchment paper was flimsy and absorbed too much of the fruit before it could start to dry. If this happens, flip it over and score the paper in the center to see if you have better luck removing the paper. To avoid this situation, use heavier parchment paper or a Silpat.

2 lb [910 g] plums, halved and pitted (skins left on)

⅓ cup [65 g] granulated sugar

Juice of ½ lemon

Line a half-sheet pan with parchment paper or a Silpat. Preheat the oven to 150°F [65°C] (or follow instructions in the headnote for alternative temperatures).

Place the plums in a food processor or blender and puree until smooth, with visible flecks of skin.

In a medium saucepan, stir together the plum puree, sugar, and lemon juice. Bring the puree to a simmer, then place a lid on top of the saucepan to partially cover it (this will help avoid splattering the stove with puree). Simmer over medium-low heat until the puree has thickened enough to coat the back of a spoon, 12 to 15 minutes. At this point, the puree will have turned a deeper color without many visible flecks of skin.

Return the puree to the food processor and blend to remove any chunks. At this point, you will have about 2½ cups [600 ml] of puree.

Pour the puree into the lined pan, shaking the pan and tapping it gently on the counter to smooth it into an even layer. (If you need to spread it out in one area, spot-treat the area with a spatula and then tap the pan again to smooth it out.) At the thickest part, it should be no more than ⅛ in [4 mm] thick.

Place the pan in the oven and leave it overnight, or until the puree peels away easily from the parchment paper while holding together, 9 to 10 hours for higher temperatures (170°F [75°C]) or 12 to 14 hours for lower temperatures. If the fruit is very sticky in the center but dry on the edges, try turning off the oven and cracking the oven door slightly to let it dry out more gently for another 30 minutes to 1 hour.

Once the sour lavash has cooled completely, remove it from the parchment paper, roll it up, and store it at room temperature in a zip-top plastic bag for up to 3 months.

Apricot Murabba

Ծիրանի մուրաբա

apricots preserved in simple syrup

When we were served tea in Armenia, we were also offered *murabba*, a fruit preserve. Not to be mistaken with jam, murabba is made up of chunks of fruit and served on little plates, the idea being that you eat a spoonful of it alongside the tea. The habit of preserving fruit in this style is common across former territories of the Persian Empire.

The tricky part was cooking the fruit in the sugar so that it didn't disintegrate into the jam. Dorothy Garabedian, an Armenian-American who lives in Germany, answered our questions by paying a visit to her eighty-year-old Armenian neighbor, Amalia Arutianz. Amalia's instructions, relayed by Dorothy, helped us write this recipe.

Start the murabba in the afternoon, let it sit for several hours, and then boil it briefly before going to sleep. Finish it in the morning. The same recipe can be used with peaches (quarter them) and sour cherries (pit them), though very fragile types of fruit, like blueberries, tend to fall apart. Green walnut, diced pumpkin, and diced eggplant murabba are also common, but they require adding lye.

-continued

Makes about 1 qt [960 g], with extra syrup

If you like to make preserves as gifts, you can put up murabba like jam and other fruit preserves in four 8 oz [240 ml] mason jars by following guidelines for water-bath processing jams available from sources such as Food in Jars (foodinjars.com). If water-bath processing, use new lids and clean jars and ensure that both the murabba and the jars are hot before filling them. When filling the jars, be mindful of air bubbles, which can get trapped below the fruit and syrup. Use a chopstick to gently move the contents of the jam around to release the air. Save leftover syrup to sweeten Kompot (page 221) or drizzle over fresh fruit.

4 cups [800 g] granulated sugar

1 cup [240 ml] water

2 lb [910 g] apricots, halved and pitted

1 lemon, for zesting

DAY ONE In a saucepan, heat the sugar and water over medium-high heat until the sugar melts, about 5 minutes.

Place the apricots in a large, heavy-bottomed pot or Dutch oven. Either grate the lemon over the apricots with a Microplane rasp or use a vegetable peeler to make strips of zest and add them to the pot. Pour the sugar syrup over the apricots and zest, ensuring that all of the pieces are coated. Place a plate directly on top of the fruit to keep the pieces submerged and prevent them from turning brown. Cover the pot for 4 to 6 hours so the fruit can macerate, releasing some of its juices.

Remove the plate, bring the pot to a boil, and then turn the heat off. Do not stir the pot, but

shake it if necessary to ensure the fruit is evenly distributed. Let the pot cool, cover, and let sit overnight.

DAY TWO The next morning, uncover and bring the apricots back to a boil, skimming and removing some foam from the top with a ladle to prevent the pot from bubbling over, but do not stir the pot—only shake it if necessary. Meanwhile, place a plate in the refrigerator to chill.

Continue to boil the apricots until the liquid has thickened to a light syrup consistency, like a true maple syrup or agave sweetener. The syrup will still look quite thin while hot, so test it by spooning some of the syrup onto the chilled plate. If it holds its shape (and looks thicker than water), it's done.

Turn off the heat and get a clean 1 qt [960 ml] mason jar or four 8 oz [240 ml] mason jars ready. Carefully ladle the apricots and syrup into the jar and leave it out, uncovered, until cooled to room temperature. If using strips of zest, you can tuck the lemon zest into the jars or discard them. Serve the murabba spooned onto a small plate to eat alongside tea, or spoon on top of yogurt. The murabba will keep for 6 to 7 months in the refrigerator.

Sweet Soujuk

Քաղցր սուջուխ

walnut-fruit "sausages"

This so-called sweet soujuk is actually the fruit-and-nut equivalent of cured sausage. Made by threading walnuts onto a string, dipping them in thickened juice (mostly grape), and then hanging them to dry until firm, it's a popular snack throughout the Caucasus. Strands of them in several colors are on full display in Yerevan's GUM market, and each vendor will offer you a taste to entice to you buy from them.

It's best to make sweet soujuk with good-quality, fresh walnut halves, which are easier to pierce with a needle without breaking. Start with a pound [455 kg] of walnuts and pick through them to get the best-looking halves and quarters, keeping in mind that some halves will break once pierced. You will likely not use all of the walnuts, but you can save the smaller pieces for Goris Baklava (page 239) or Gata (page 235). Once the walnuts are strung, you'll dip the strands into the thickened juice as if you were making a wax candle—and when they're dry, the soujuks do look a little like wax.

-continued

Makes 5 soujuks about 12 in [30.5 cm] long

Before starting, locate a cool, dry place to hang the soujuks while drying (which takes between 3 and 5 days). There is no single way to do this, and the first time can be tricky. One solution is to find a place to hang a clean clothes hanger and place a tray underneath to catch any drips. Before dipping the soujuks, tie the string at the top of each strand in a loop. Next, partially open up a paper clip on one end so it resembles the hook on a Christmas ornament and thread the other end of the paper clip through the loop. This way, once you've dipped a soujuk strand in the thickened juice, you can then hang it from the paperclip on the clothes hanger. For the sauce, you can make your own grape juice by blending and straining fresh grapes, but store-bought grape juice works fine, too. Look for grape juice with no added sugar. Grape molasses is available at Middle Eastern grocery stores.

1 lb [455 g] walnut halves and quarters

2 cups [440 ml] grape juice

¾ cup [180 ml] grape molasses

¼ cup [50 g] granulated sugar

¼ tsp ground allspice

Pinch of ground cinnamon

Pinch of ground nutmeg

⅓ cup [45 g] all-purpose flour

⅓ cup [45 g] cornstarch

1½ cups [360 ml] water

Before stringing the walnuts, find a sturdy sewing needle (it doesn't have to be unusually thick or large, but you want one that doesn't bend when piercing the walnut pieces). Cut a piece of sewing thread slightly longer than 3 ft [92 cm] long, thread the needle, and double back on the thread once to make it a bit longer than 1½ ft

[46 cm]. Tie a knot at the end. To thread the walnuts, pierce them in the center so that the pieces stack snugly together like beads on a necklace with only the thin sides of the walnuts exposed. If there are no more halves or quarters, make use of the biggest broken pieces. Thread each strand until it is about 12 in [30.5 cm] long, and leave at least 6 in [15 cm] of thread at the top to make it easier to hang the soujuk once it's dipped.

To make the dipping sauce, in a saucepan or small pot, bring the grape juice, grape molasses, sugar, allspice, cinnamon, and nutmeg to a gentle simmer. In a bowl, whisk together flour, cornstarch, and 1 cup [240 ml] water. While mixing, slowly pour the water-starch mixture into the grape juice and mix well until the sauce is smooth. Stir in the remaining ½ cup [120 ml] water and continue to heat the sauce while stirring constantly for 2 minutes. The sauce will thicken up quickly, becoming opaque enough to completely coat the end of a wooden spoon.

Turn the heat off. While the sauce is still warm, dip a walnut strand into the pot, using a spatula or wooden spoon to press the walnuts into the sauce to submerge them, but hold on to the end of the string so it stays dry. The sauce should coat the walnuts completely. Lift the walnut strand out of the sauce and pause for a moment to let any excess sauce drip into the pot. Hang the strand and repeat with the remaining strands. (If the mixture becomes too thick to coat the walnuts, turn the heat to low and stir in a little water to loosen it up).

Let the soujuk strands hang in a cool, dry place (preferably no hotter than 70°F [21°C]) for 3 to 5 days, or until dry to the touch. Before eating, cut the bottom end of the soujuk strand and pull out the thread from the top end. If the thread gets stuck in places, just cut the soujuk where it is stuck to release it. It's okay if each soujuk doesn't stay in one piece. Soujuks keeps for up to 2 months at room temperature in a tightly sealed container. To serve, slice the soujuk crosswise into coins or larger chunks.

Halva

Հալվա

stovetop shortbread

Not to be mistaken with Middle Eastern *halva* made with sesame seeds, halva in Armenia is made with flour and butter and tastes like shortbread cookies with the texture of fudge, the perfect thing to eat with a cup of *soorj*. Traditionally, the rich snack was given to new mothers so they could regain their strength. In Yerevan, Astghik Gyonjyan patiently walked us through the steps on how to reach the optimal balance of flour, butter, sugar, and salt—and it does take some patience, starting with stirring the flour and butter together over the stove for at least 15 minutes until it reaches a shade of light gold. Astghik makes hers on the lighter side, but if you prefer a deeper, peanut butter–like color, simply cook the flour and butter together longer before adding the sugar.

A couple of tips before you start: Don't use a cast-iron Dutch oven the first time you make halva. Although it shaves off some of the cooking time, there is less wiggle room when mixing in the sugar before it starts to caramelize and burn. Also, this recipe includes a step for clarifying the butter, which removes milk solids and water and prevents the butter from burning. You can clarify and then refrigerate the butter several days in advance. If buying clarified butter, you can skip the first step.

-continued

Makes sixteen 2 in [5 cm] pieces

1¼ cups [275 g] unsalted butter (or ¾ cup [180 ml] clarified butter)

2½ cups [350 g] all-purpose flour

¾ cup [150 g] granulated sugar

½ tsp kosher salt

To make the clarified butter, melt the butter in a small pot over low heat for 20 to 25 minutes. (This can be done on the weakest burner on the stove.) Line a strainer with muslin or cheesecloth (if you have either) and place it over a heatproof bowl. Using a ladle, skim and discard the frothy white solids that rise to the surface of the butter. Once all the solids have been removed, ladle the clear, melted butter through the strainer, stopping before you get to the layer at the bottom of the pot, which is a mix of milk solids and water. If a little water or milk solids remain in the butter, that's okay—it won't ruin the halva.

Have a pie tin or an 8 in [20 cm] square pan ready. You can line the pan with parchment paper to make it easier to transfer the halva out of the pan, but it's optional.

To make the halva, in a wide, heavy-bottomed saucepan, heat the butter over medium-high heat until it begins to shimmer. (If there is still some water in the butter, it will start to sputter, and that's okay.) Lower the heat to medium and stir in the flour with a sturdy spoon or spatula. Continue stirring, lowering the heat any time the flour smells toasted or starts to turn brown too quickly in places, for about 18 minutes. It will seem dry at the beginning but toward the end it will turn into a soft Play-Doh consistency. If after 18 minutes the flour is as pale as cream,

continue to cook, stirring constantly, until the flour takes on a more golden appearance. Alternatively, if by 15 minutes the flour is already darkening to a caramel color, turn off the heat and stir to prevent the flour from burning, then proceed to the next step.

Once the flour is a light caramel color and the butter begins rising to the surface of the flour, making it look shiny, turn off the heat and vigorously stir in the sugar and salt to form a uniform paste and to avoid bits of sugar clumping together.

Transfer the paste to the prepared pan. Smooth the top by tapping the back of a spoon against the surface or using an offset spatula. If the surface looks oily, blot it dry with a couple of paper towels. Use a fork to make a crisscross pattern across the top, then cut into squares or diamonds about 2 in [5 cm] long.

Let cool completely before serving. Halva keeps in an airtight container at room temperature for up to 2 weeks.

Gata

Գ ա թ

"coffee cake" with walnuts

A not-too-sweet baked good served with coffee or tea, *gata* is made by enclosing a butter-and-flour filling with dough—most of the time. No two gata are alike: Some are made with a yeasted dough and baked in a tonir while some are made into individual portions, almost like scones. And some—like this one—are filled with nuts. This rendition was inspired by Alex Ghazaryan, chef at the Tufenkian Old Dilijan Complex. He learned how to make it by watching his grandmother, who, like most bakers in Armenia, measured everything *achkachap*—by the eye. While we watched, he shaped the soft, pliable dough into what looked like a large dumpling filled with butter, sugar, and walnuts before pressing it into a disk, never once using a rolling pin. We've reengineered it to fit standard measurements in America, but the low-tech spirit of the dessert—and the rich walnut filling—is true to the original.

A few notes before you start: Handle the dough gently so it doesn't become tough once it's baked. Read the shaping method before you start so you can anticipate the shape you'll need to create to form the gata. In some cases, the filling may bubble out of part of the gata as it bakes. Don't worry, it will still taste good.

-continued

Makes one 9 in [23 cm] cake

DOUGH

¼ cup [60 g] unsalted butter, at room temperature

⅓ cup plus 1 Tbsp [80 g] granulated sugar

½ cup [120 g] plain, whole-milk yogurt

¼ cup [60 g] sour cream

1 tsp kosher salt

¼ tsp baking soda

1¾ cups [245 g] all-purpose flour, plus more for dusting

FILLING

2 Tbsp unsalted butter, at room temperature

½ cup [55 g] walnuts, lightly toasted and chopped

⅓ cup [65 g] granulated sugar

1½ Tbsp all-purpose flour

¼ tsp kosher salt (optional)

1 large egg, lightly beaten

Preheat the oven to 375°F [190°C]. Line a half-sheet pan with parchment paper or lightly oil it. Have one large bowl and two medium bowls handy.

To make the dough, in a medium bowl, mash and mix the butter and sugar together with a rubber spatula until they form a paste.

In the large bowl, mix together the yogurt, sour cream, salt, and baking soda with a spoon or rubber spatula. Add the butter and sugar to the yogurt and mix well. It's okay if the butter and sugar aren't blended completely into the yogurt.

Gradually stir in the flour with the rubber spatula. Once the flour is incorporated, gently knead the dough with your hands, patting it into the bowl with the palm of your hand and folding it over itself inside the bowl until the dough is soft and smooth.

Dust the counter with flour and place the dough on top. Gently knead a couple of times, dusting with flour to keep it from sticking, until it is only slightly tacky when touched. Pat the dough into a disk about 6 in [15 cm] wide, place on a plate, and refrigerate while you make the filling. (This makes the dough less sticky and easier to handle.)

To make the filling, in the remaining medium bowl, use your hands to mix together the butter, walnuts, sugar, flour, and salt, if using.

To shape and bake, dust the counter with flour and place the dough on top. Using your fingers, gently press the dough into a 10 in [25 cm] round, leaving the center of the round slightly domed and the edges thinner. Place the filling in the center, leaving a 1½ in [4 cm] edge. Gather the edges up over the filling and pleat and press together as if sealing a large, round dumpling. Press firmly to seal the edges so the filling is no longer exposed. Flatten the dough gently with the palm of your hand to smooth any edges and ensure that the gata is sealed.

Place the gata, sealed-side down, in the center of the lined pan and press firmly with the palm of your hand to flatten into an 8 in [20 cm] round.

With the flat side of a fork's tines (and not the sharp points), press lines across the top of the

-continued

gata in a crisscross pattern. Brush the top and sides generously with the beaten egg and then bake, rotating the pan halfway through, until the top is golden brown but before the bottom is dark brown, about 30 minutes. (It may look lighter than in the photo on page 237.)

Let cool completely on the sheet pan. Cut into wedges for serving. Gata is best the day it's baked. Reheat day-old gata slices in a toaster oven before serving. Alternatively, freeze the finished gata and reheat at 350°F [180°C] until hot in the center.

Goris Baklava

Գորիսի փախլավա

Forget familiar filo-pastry baklava; with three layers of short-crust pastry interspersed with meringue, the only thing this version has in common with the former is the walnuts. This is also what makes this recipe so appealing—you can make the dough at home and it bakes up to be a sturdy pastry with walnuts and meringue melding together for a chewy filling surrounded by flaky crust. This style of baklava comes from the southern corner of Armenia around Goris, and Anahit Badalyan, who also prepared many dishes for us using Goris's famous beans (see page 114), showed us how to make it.

Before you start, separate three eggs, allocating two yolks for the dough, one yolk for the egg wash, and all of the egg whites for the filling. For baking the baklava, a glass 9 by 13 in [23 by 33 cm] casserole dish works well (jelly-roll pans and quarter-sheet pans are too shallow). While the beaten egg whites are described as meringue in the method, it isn't intended to bake up like meringue—rather, it nearly dissolves into the walnuts, sweetening the pastry. Drizzling honey at the end gives a final sweet accent to a pastry that isn't overly sweet to begin with.

-continued

Makes about twenty-four 2 in [5 cm] pieces

DOUGH

2¾ cups [370 g] all-purpose flour, plus more for dusting

¾ cup plus 1 Tbsp [185 g] cold unsalted butter, cubed

¾ cup [180 g] plain, whole-milk yogurt

2 large egg yolks

1 tsp kosher salt

½ tsp baking soda

FILLING

2 heaping cups [220 g] walnuts

3 large egg whites

1 tsp pure vanilla extract

1⅓ cups [265 g] granulated sugar

TOPPING

1 large egg yolk

2 Tbsp honey

To make the dough, in a large bowl, add the flour and butter. Using the palms of your hands and your fingers, rub the butter into the flour until the pieces are no larger than a chickpea.

In a small bowl, mix the yogurt, egg yolks, salt, and baking soda together with a fork.

Make a deep well in the center of the flour and pour in the yogurt mixture. Using a fork, mix the flour into the yogurt to form a shaggy dough. With the palm of your hand, press the dough into the base of the bowl, then fold it and press it again into the base of the bowl. Repeat a couple of times until the dough starts to come together.

Dust the counter with flour and place the dough on top. Pat it flat and fold it over itself, repeating a couple of times until nearly smooth. The dough should feel soft and pliable. If it feels very dry, sprinkle a few drops of water over it with your hands and let it rest for a few minutes before kneading again.

Cut the dough into three equal pieces. Pull off a golf ball–size piece from one and add it to another so you have a small, medium, and large portion. Dust the counter with more flour, place the portions side by side on top of the flour, and use your hands to shape each portion into a rectangle (this makes rolling them into a rectangle easier). Place a clean kitchen towel over the dough pieces and let them rest while making the filling. (If your kitchen is hot and the dough feels sticky, refrigerate it for 30 minutes to make it easier to handle.)

To make the filling, place the walnuts on a cutting board and place a sheet of parchment paper on top. Roll and press a rolling pin over the paper, rocking it back and forth, to break the walnuts into smaller pieces. Remove the paper and chop the larger pieces with a knife. (It's okay if the sizes are not uniform.)

In a stand mixer fitted with the whisk attachment or with a handheld mixer, whip the egg whites until frothy, about 30 seconds. Add the vanilla and sugar and whip on medium-high speed until the meringue forms ribbons when it drips off the whisk, 2 to 3 minutes.

-continued

To assemble and bake, place a rack in the center of the oven and preheat the oven to 350°F [180°C]. Lightly coat a 9 by 13 in [23 by 33 cm] casserole pan with butter and line with parchment paper.

Dust the counter with flour. Roll out the medium-size piece of dough until it's large enough to cover the base of the prepared pan. Lift the dough into the pan and press it into the corners, trimming any excess dough along the edges to help it fit.

Spread half of the meringue across the dough in the pan in an even layer, ensuring that it reaches the corners, and isn't mounded in the center (this will ensure the meringue doesn't puff up too much in the middle more than the sides). Cover the meringue with half of the walnuts and press the walnuts lightly into the meringue. Roll out the smallest piece of dough into a rectangle large enough to cover the first layer. Lift it into the pan and press down lightly, trimming away any excess dough. Spread the remaining meringue over the top, ensuring it reaches the corners and isn't mounded in the center, followed by the remaining walnuts. Roll out the largest layer of dough into a rectangle large enough to cover the top (it will be a little thicker than the other two). Place it on top of the walnut layer and trim away any excess dough on the edges. Refrigerate the baklava for 20 to 30 minutes (this will make it easier to cut).

With a sharp knife pointed at a near 90-degree angle following the length of the pan, cut the baklava lengthwise into four strips, wiping the blade of the knife in between cuts and ensuring that the cuts go through all of the layers. Then cut the dough at a diagonal across the pan at 2 in [5 cm] intervals to create diamonds. You will end up with about 24 diamond-shaped pieces and some smaller pieces at the ends.

For the topping, break up the remaining yolk with a fork and gently brush it over the surface of the baklava.

Bake for 35 to 40 minutes, rotating the pan halfway through, or until the top is golden brown. Remove from the oven and run a knife through the cuts to keep the pieces from sticking together. Drizzle the honey over the top and return to the oven for 8 to 10 minutes to ensure the center of the pan cooks through. Cool completely before serving. Baklava keeps in an airtight container at room temperature for up to 5 days.

Acknowledgments

The kernel of this book idea originated in an email in spring 2015 from Eric Grigorian to John Lee, asking if he'd consider leading a food photography workshop for kids in Armenia through an organization called TUMO. It was through this connection that we met the organization's director, Marie Lou Papazian, her husband and advisory board member, Pegor Papazian, their dynamic family, and the impressive and generous network of TUMO-ians across the world (thank you, Eric).

It is no understatement that this project never would have happened if Marie Lou and Pegor hadn't paved the way for us countless times, including our unforgettable trip to Artsakh and Lake Sevan with Marie Lou and our sunrise journey to the genocide memorial with Pegor. We are also forever grateful that Marie Lou and Pegor were able to fight through road blocks to bring John to a hospital after his legs were wounded by a stun grenade at a protest during the 2018 Velvet Revolution.

A big thanks to the countless TUMO-ians who helped along the way, especially: Tatevik Avakyan, Knar Babayan, Samvel Berkibekyan, Zara Budaghyan, Nara Davtian, Saten Grigoryan, Astghik Hambardzumyan, Mariam Metcpagian Zakarian, Maral Mikirditsian, Anna Mkrtchyan, and Lilit Tovmasyan.

A special thanks to Tania Sahakian for connecting John with Ara as we started to research this book.

Our trips in Armenia covered a lot of ground, and for that we are indebted to the translating and insider expertise of Christine Goroyan and Raffi Youredjian, who put up with our many lame lavash puns. Thanks also to Christine for her translation help once we were in California. You guys are forever part of Team Lavash.

Our research brought us into the homes, restaurants, and workplaces of many people in Armenia, where we were shown the kind of hospitality that we'd have only expected if we were family. Thanks to: Gayane Arevshatyan; Jirair Avanian; Grigor Avetissyan; Manoush Avetisyan; Anahit Badalyan and daughter Sona; Vahe Baloulian; Hasmik Bughdaryan; Nara Davtian; Ani Harutyunyan; Emma Harutunyan and family; Lilia Harutyunyan and daughter Mariam; Rita Harutyunyan; Stepan Garaghanyan; Alex Ghazaryan; Robert Ghazaryan; Ghegham Grigoryan; Varduhi Grigoryan; Astghik Gyonjyan; Shake Havan-Garapetyan; Alla Hayrapetyan; Samvel Hayrapetyan; Vahe Keushguerian and daughter Aimee; Arpine Manukyan; Armenuhi Marukyan; Armen Qefilyan; Mariam Saghatelyan; Armine Simonyan; Anna Tatosyan and employees, including Lusine Abrahamyan, Aida Beyboutyan, Liana Grigoryan, Nara Ivanyan, and Hasmik Khachatryan; Yervand Taderosyan; Zak and Arsineh Valladian; and Armine Yeghiazaryan.

Thanks to Halle Butvin for believing in this project from our first chat in Yerevan, for inviting us to the 2018 Smithsonian Folklife Festival in Washington, D.C., and for the inspiration behind our chapter titles. Thanks also to the support of Sabrina Lynn Motley and Jackie Pangelinan for making us feel like part of the festival.

Thanks to the many who helped in our research quest when we were home in California, whether it was by finding books and primary sources, answering our many cooking and culture questions, helping us track down recipes, or supporting us in myriad other ways while we wrote the book. Thanks to: David Adelsheim; Noubar Afeyan; Sossie Atallah; Christine Avakoff; Sara Bir; Christine Gallary; Dorothy Garabedian; Darra Goldstein; Clémence Gossett; Mari Guedikian; Harry Henien; Roman Hovsepyan; Roxana Jullapat; Shushan Karapetian; Ellen King; Kathryn Lukas; Kara Plikaitis; Sona Makalian; Tatev Malkhasyan; Marisa McClellan; Andrea Nguyen; the Sargsyan family, including Varduhi, Benik, Ashkhen, Ashot, Armine Gabrielyan, and Johan Gregorian; Karen Scholthof; Molly Stevens; Barbara Sutton; Alanna Taylor-Tobin; Ruzanna Tsaturyan; Karen Zada; and Maggie Zada.

Thanks to our enthusiastic group of volunteer testers and proofreaders. You truly helped us hone our recipes with smart feedback and candid questions. Thanks to: Sandy Binder, Grace Bishop, Bebe Black Carminito, Hannah Davitian, Aaron Herbert, Ching-Yee Hu, Michael Ingram, Diana Kerian,

-continued

Jennifer Sackett, Mary Ann Shattuck, Sandra Wu, and Annelies Zjiderveld.

At Chronicle, a special thanks to our editor, Sarah Billingsley, for seeing the potential in our book from the beginning and being there when we needed it at the end. Thanks to the entire team at Chronicle, including Rachel Harrell for our book design, Margo Winton Parodi for copyediting, Mikayla Butchart, Karen Levy, and Cecilia Santini for proofreading, Joyce Lin for publicity, Cynthia Shannon for marketing, Magnolia Molcan for editorial oversight, and Tera Kilip and Steve Kim for production. And to Alice Chau for traveling with Team Lavash in Yerevan.

Thanks to Shaunt Berberian for pitching in with an incredible map of Armenia at the final hour.

Our book never would have happened had it not been for the positive feedback and frank conversations with our agent, Amy Collins, who envisioned our title before we had written a word. (Remember when we called it *Bread, Bones, and Barbecue?*) Thank you.

PERSONAL THANKS:

From John: To my wife Jen for supporting me while I went swashbuckling through Armenia over the years. Ilubb.

From Ara: To my Nene, without your guidance I wouldn't be who I am today.

From Kate: To the Leahy family for letting us take over the house for a photo shoot, and to Patrick Kim for (once again) letting me get flour all over the place.

For the sources used to research this book, please visit lavashthebook.com.

Index